Stung by Salt and War

# Reading Plus

Mary Ann Caws, General Editor

Vol. 2

PETER LANG
New York · Bern · Frankfurt am Main · Paris

Richard J. Pioli

# Stung by Salt and War

## Creative Texts of the Italian Avant-Gardist F. T. Marinetti

PETER LANG
New York · Bern · Frankfurt am Main · Paris

**Library of Congress Cataloging-in-Publication Data**

**Marinetti, Filippo Tommaso, 1876-1944.**
 Stung by salt and war.

 (Reading plus ; vol. 2)
 Bibliography: p.
 1. Marinetti, Filippo Tommaso, 1876-1944—Translations,
English. I. Pioli, Richard J., 1953-    . II. Title. III. Series.
PQ4829.A76A25  1987         858′.91209         86-27286
 ISBN 0-8204-0381-4
 ISSN 0882-6196


CIP-Kurztitelaufnahme der Deutschen Bibliothek

**Pioli, Richard J.:**
Stung by salt and war: creative texts of the
Italian avant-gardist F.T. Marinetti / Richard
J. Pioli – New York; Bern; Frankfurt am Main;
Paris: Lang, 1987.
 (Reading plus; Vol. 2)
 ISBN 0-8204-0381-4


NE: GT

Printed by Weihert-Druck GmbH, Darmstadt, West Germany

TABLE OF CONTENTS

PREFACE

   The most refined move of the entire futurist chess game
was perhaps the opening one, the choice of a name.  In opting
for Futurism precisely, and rejecting Dynamism, according to
one of the myths hovering around the beginnings of the first
European avant-garde, Filippo Tommaso Marinetti obliged his
adversary to make a series of counter-moves that would have
ended with transforming him--more or less inevitably--into
an ideal accomplice, into the sulky and compliant victim of
an unredeemed and irredeemable love, of a passion which ages
without maturing.  The antagonist is implicated, but the rules
of the game are dictated unilaterally.  Instead of being flat-
tered the reader is invaded; rather than being seduced, he is
literally occupied and colonized, and every one of his pleas-
ures is spied on from the vantage point of an imperious cate-
chizing will.  After decades of homiletic literature and oleo-
graphs, who would ever have been able--or wanted--to withdraw
from the delirium implicit in this perennial dissatisfaction?
Who would ever have thought in cold blood to renounce this
bed where every lament makes itself understood as the presage
of new delicious torments?
   All the same, it was inevitable that sooner or later
Futurism would reveal its true archeological calling and that
the exasperated iconoclasm of its masks would begin to acquire
tonality and nostalgic shadings.  Naturally this was not a
question of ideological consumption, of changed circumstances,
of new gods issuring forth from who knows what unforeseeable
horizons.  It was (and is even now) a question internal to
the dynamics of Futurism's promises.  The making of the future,
in fact, is an inaccessible undertaking, except on the condition of forgetting the future itself in the moment in which
it becomes present, and thus an object of experience.  The
unique condition in which the future can truly be enjoyed
would imply a total cancellation of memory, even that, we
must agree, of the future perfect.  There is no way to sink
into a science fiction dream without immediately associating
with archetypally expressive forms, with narrative resolu-
tions having mythopoetic origins.  And there is more: it is
not possible to predict the future without acknowledging at
the same time the obsolescence of one's own images.
   The uneasiness that results from this certainly has to
do with what Marinetti and his followers meant by the cult
of speed and which we today tend rather to experience as a
paradox.  The constant acceleration of every moment seems
not so much to conduce to a breaking open of the notion of
time but rather to a flattening out of perception.  The result is a decided paradigmatic impoverishment: the grid of
possibilities tends to create compulsion.  Before this blind
alley in which Futurism meant to chase itself, there remained

only two interesting possibilities: the imperturbable renunciation (participation in entropy) challenged or re-
proached by the use of a rationalistic type of logos, and
the pretense of an obsessive mania; or the play of extrem-
ity, of a lay religion (constructivist) propped up by the
adoption of stubborn glossolalic stylistic traits. Luckily
for us, Marinetti preferred the latter temptation.

It is to the undisputed merit of the author of this
collection to have intuited that "The machines of Marinetti's imaginative writings cannot be said to bear such
close resemblances to real machines, although this was
his intention. They are also sometimes as fanciful as
Duchamp's machines and allow an interpretation of them as
metaphors of enthusiasm and hope." I don't know how far
I would know how to follow Richard Pioli on the level of
interpretation, but I am one hundred percent convinced that
the type of metaphoric reading he proposes is the right one.
Right for us, and clearly the most fruitful.

If I spoke at the beginning of a game of chess, of a
master/slave relationship, if I obliquely suggested the
compulsion to repeat, it was to arrive here, at this hypo-
thesis, until today sacrificed on the altar of encounter
(presumed) with reality (presumed): the profile of history,
the torment of ideological responsibility, etc. Nailed by
the expectations of similar critical mortifications, Futurism
has endured much. That little which is known in the English
language is certainly vitiated by motivations of amazement
or, which comes to the same thing, by bourgeois supercilious-
ness. The texts translated up to now have been chosen,
furthermore, as the most reassuring.

There is then a second invaluable merit of Richard
Pioli--that of presenting an exceptionally attentive and
attention worthy range of works which follow the entire parabola of Marinetti's evolution. Each reader may select
among the pages of this book the moment that is for him
the most appropriate for entering·the game. Just remember
that in order to play it is necessary to accept the form
of the game and to choose from its contents. A final
warning: don't be alarmed if the game is a sado-masochistic
one.

Luigi Ballerini

New York City

1986

# INTRODUCTION

Filippo Tommaso Marinetti, in dramatic contrast to the literary principles which dominated his time, promoted a new writing. This writing wanted to liberate expression but it also allied itself to a ruthless materialism of words that glorified technology and a new age. The manifestos he produced and deftly publicized, with their vivid scenarios of confrontation, redefined the role of art from the privileged perspective of a machine-visionary. In concentrating upon revealing those forms which would allow all kinds of human activity to be seen as art, he easily appeared possessed by his own neologistic furor and by that swagger that underscored his cosmopolitan drive, a drive that was absurdly ludic and a very essential ingredient. These forms he packaged with sporadic vulgarity while he also proposed much more seriously a claim to the actual as his terrain and to the eternal as a dream incapacitating a human being's necessary intuition of his time and of a time to come. The redirection of culture on a global level necessitated the presence of such an early enthusiast of the concept of art as an instrument of revolution.

In the beginning the Futurists most certainly made great shock waves but, always running up against the built-in certainty of their own obsolescence as did every subsequent avant-garde movement, they found themselves unable to continuously create better innovations. They struggled to push beyond a disruptive attitude toward a more serious exploration of their own sensory violence with its nihilistic results. In this they failed. Their radical reorientation of artistic taste, so large a step, seemed too preoccupied with their mere reacting to "passéist" critics.

Marinetti dismissed Nietzsche as passéist. By describing him in the 1913 manifesto on Variety Theater as climbing the mountain peaks of Thessaly while fettered with his gigantic Greek texts, Marinetti displays a clever, pugnacious style taught to him by Nietzsche himself, a genuine predecessor. Another example as disruptive is Marinetti's assertion that The Divine Comedy is a "rats' nest of commentators."

Marinetti programmatically utilized intuition and instinct and humorously belittled reason and sentiment, although of course many romantic aspects contradictorally flourished. He preached that generations were to build their own cities and in turn raze them so as not to be outlived by their makers; new men would replace the Futurists themselves and a forever new "dynamism" would come to grow in the newly-made clearings. Commenting on the aversion to any trace of the Absolute, Futurist Ardengo Soffici remarked that he found the Moulin Rouge much more fascinating.

Filippo Tommaso Marinetti (Philippe Achille Emile, whose mother called him Tommaso) was an Italian born in Alexandria in 1876. He was immersed in French culture and began his career in Paris, from where he went on be "part lyrical genius, part organ grinder, and...part Fascist demagogue."[1] His voluminous 'oeuvre' includes the first Italian translations of Mallarmé; epic, lyric and vers libre poetry; an "explosive novel"; words in freedom, synoptic and freeword tableaux or broadsheets; aeropoetry and simultaneous poetry; manifestos on art, politics, society morality and literature; radio performances, plays, cabaret, variety theater, songs and letters. He co-authored the first Italian aerial dictionary in 1929 and embedded within this novel achievement is an acknowledgement of the importance of new technological language for the country that creates it.

The Press dubbed him "the caffeine of Europe" which gives the impression that he was indeed the very embodiment of the Futurist "art-life" creed. His friendship, enthusiasm and generosity are known to have propelled every cause of the movement and this disposition regarding how to make art important in life bears the trace of total commitment that we can find in another modernist vitality, that of Ezra Pound.

Before the cultural theology of Futurism was established, Marinetti experimented with a variety of metrical styles, precepts established in Paris by Rene Ghil and Gustave Khan. His background actually includes all the significant artistic and extra-artistic ideas then in vogue all over Europe. Standing upon the portal of a new century, Marinetti drew from Zola, Whitman, Verhaeren, the French Symbolists, Bergson, Sorel, Nietzsche, D'Annunzio and Pascoli. Giovanni Papini and Giuseppe Prezzolini, the directors from 1903 to 1907 of the Florentine review Leonardo, often praised important audacious deeds and the need for action. They too inspired Marinetti.

After Marinetti's parents sent him from his home in Alexandria in 1893 to study in Paris he began to frequent the literary goings-on then in full swing. Being sensitive to them, he proceeded to write compositions that were symbolist-inspired, then went on to become a propagandist in Italy for symbolism. With translations, the conferences and lectures he carried to other cities, Marinetti popularized Mallarmé, Rimbaud, Verlaine, Maeterlinck, Khan and others. He wrote for Anthologie-Revue, La Critique internationale, La Vogue, La Revue blanche, Vers et Prose, and in 1904 began to publish Poesia, a review designed to further strengthen cultural ties. His cosmopolitan attitude is unusual and unique, if one considers the ordinary route of most authors: that they become nourished by foreign literature only after knowing their native culture.

As a journalist, Marinetti was indispensable in relaying important poetic ideas to his Italian audience. In his series of articles for La Vogue in 1899 entitled "The Poetic Movement in Italy," he wrote that Italian poetry had not developed since the days of Leopardi, that it had remained empty of the modern spirit. It was Parnassian. He proposed to clear away its provincialism.

Mallarmé influenced the young poet, but, whether through an inability to grasp the great poet's complexities or as the result of a willful modification, Marinetti developed a poetic approach consisting of exact, comparative terms, "intuitions" which brought distant things into relations. Between 1897 and 1909 he worked, camoflaging at times, with his writings' many influences. Their surface is resplendent with Whitman-like lyricism and he often takes his inspiration from the sea, an image of great power and infinitude. "Fanfare of the Waves" was published in 1902 in La conquête des étoiles (Conquest of the Stars), a "poème epique" of nineteen vers libre cantos. The revelry of the grotesque images and the eternal conflict is more akin to allegory than symbolist suggestion:

> O sorceresses of the Impossible! Stars!
> Promisers of nothing! There you are,
>     before me
> within reach of my vengeance! Oh my joy!
> Oh! that I may savor the unbridled
>     drunkeness
> of spitting on your majestic faces!
> Victory is certain, know it!
> The victory is ours; we will be ten
>     million
> Waves at the assault of your metal walls!

Earth has summoned a Luciferian apocalypse with the total destruction of the heavens. The victors anticipate the death of god and the new reign of a coming "overman." In his later 'roman,' Le monoplan du pape (The Pope's Monoplane), Marinetti sought to express by similarly energetic means the nullity of the pope. He went on to condemn moonlight in his second Futurist manifesto, "Uccidiamo il chiaro di luna" ("Let's Murder the Moonlight"), the formidable opponent on the side of romanticism hanging high in the sky above melancholy Venice, that "great sewer of passéism."

At the conference on poetry and vers libre in 1908, promoted by the review Poesia, Futurist Paolo Buzzi described intuition and poetic innovation. Later, his idea would become a major Futurist principle:

> A general stress (which directs an entire
> sentence in conversation) in declamation
> directs an entire strophe and establishes
> the measure of values heard. Such a stress
> (similar in essence for the whole world, in
> the sense that all passions produce very
> nearly the same phenomenon of increase or
> decrease) is communicated to the words by
> means of the sentiment stirring the speaker
> or poet uniquely, whatever the tonic accent
> or fixed value the same words could them-
> selves delimit. The stress of this impulse
> directs the harmony of the principle verse
> which imprints movement on the developed
> idea. And the other verses, unless an ef-
> fect of contrast is sought, must be modelled
> upon the values of the first...This stress
> and its watchful appropriation of itself
> to the importance and the temporary nature
> of the sentiment evoked, or of the sensation
> to be translated, is what releases all the
> dominating energies through song...But the
> most important fact is this: that a similar
> technique enables every poet, of every lan-
> guage, to formulate his verse or, rather,
> his original strophe: to write his own
> characteristic, personal rhythm instead of
> wearing, so to speak, an already-worn uni-
> form which would reduce him to being the
> pupil of a glorious predecessor, even in the
> best of cases. 2

The importance of vers libre for Marinetti was that it possessed the perpetual dynamism of thought. For him it opened like a window upon the tendencies of the modern world. In giving the appropriate rhythm to each word, vers libre became the major form for him and his followers. By importing it to Italy, Marinetti claimed to be the libera- tor of Italian poetry. He declaimed his poetry from stages everywhere and there are many who have testified to the pro- foundly felt value of his syllables. Effects drawn from conversation, oratory, and theater can be inferred from imagining the recitiation of the poem "To My Pegasus," from the still pre-Futurist work, Le ville charnelle (The Carnal City) of 1908. The poet's lyric mania and admiration for his modern, hungry automobile are vividly drawn using suspension points to convey the wild, rhythmical, staccato-like flow of images:

> Mountains with fresh cloaks of turquoise!...
> Beautiful rivers breathing in the moonlight!...
> Shadowy plains!  I can overtake you
> with a grand gallop on this enraged monster...
> Stars, my Stars, do you hear its steps,
> the baying crash and interminable collapsing
> of its metal lungs?
>
> I accept the bet...  with you, my Stars!...
> Faster!...  Faster still!...
> Constantly, without a rest!...
> Loosen the reins!...  You can't?...
> Then crush them!...
> So the motor's pulse heaves a hundred times
>          harder!

On September 18, 1886, the "Manifeste symboliste" of Jean Moréas had been published in Le Figaro and similarly the "Futurist Manifesto" was published in Le Figaro on February 20, 1909.  There too Marinetti describes a violent automobile with its zealous driver, and again celebrates a flight from reason into the unknown.  The car overturns in a ditch, barely avoiding hitting two cyclists.  He is jubilant over the rebirth that follows: the car is lifted out of the mud, still able to run but with its "coachwork of common sense" and its "soft upholstery of convenience" discarded, as if they had been punished for their ornamental hollowness.  What remains is the hard body of the machine, appealing for its simple embodiment of action for its own sake.

Marinetti advocated "modernolatry," the adoration of machines, as the answer to established culture and its past. Faith was to replenish itself with technology and an esthetic of the machine.  With this the movement began to present the image of themselves as nurturing and developing a public taste for modern culture's contents.

The machines of Marinetti's imaginative writings cannot be said to bear such close resemblances to real machines, although this was his intention.  They are also sometimes as fanciful as Duchamp's machines and allow an interpretation of them as metaphors of enthusiasm and hope.  When both aspects collide, we are witnesses to a strange amalgam of precision language as Marinetti explains it in the technical manifestos and a wild, funny fantasy of outlandish, mechanized monsters.

The prophetic, utopian announcement of revolution in civilization joined the transcendental promise Marinetti found in the machine. The poets of the movement (Libero Altomare, Mario Betuda, Paolo Buzzi, Enrico Cavacchioli, Auro D'Alba, Luciano Folgore, Corrado Govoni, Aldo Palazzeschi among the first generation, and others later), produced promethean works and summoned great power for themselves as Rimbaud, Lautréamont and Mallarmé had shown all poets when they invoked their own divine wills. The Futurists tried to show man's obsolescence and why he must be transcended. They also unknowingly prefigured the destructive gestures of later so-called liberators by glorifying militarism and patriotism. Although Marinetti was initially in pursuit of a worldwide movement, somewhere along the line he succumbed to this nationalistic attitude which in turn became a form of anarchic-fascism.

The war on society which the Futurists waged may not appear like much of a class war, a conflict between the bourgeosie and the proletariat. Theirs was rather a war between those who could start an Italian cultural revolution and those who had to submit to its conception and realization. In the realm of politics where the movement also had interests, the negation of the class war for the sake of the country's larger benefits would later be known as a gesture enacted by the imperialist political bourgeoisie which in turn developed Fascism.3

Futurists reacted to the typical Italian evils of 'bella forma,' lavish description and the cult of the 'I' in a war-like way; with these they waged a kind of war. In 1911, Marinetti described Italians as dwellers trapped in a museum with their inheritance of Greco-Roman antiquity. This is easily observed by all who march along the Grand Tour, even during our own time, and we must confess that it is a condition unlike that in most other countries. One muses over the possible influence the United States had for Marinetti who never visited them. How much did the idea of a place with a great future, about to be built with steel, which held Marinetti's attention, how much did it evolve out of myths about America?

The tenth article of the founding Manifesto longs for the destruction of "museums, the libraries, the academies of every kind." Again it may be feeble to assert that in real terms Marinetti did not mean this, but the question now, in light of subsequent history, becomes a matter of the bond between politics and culture. Can we ever see them as separate entities again? For the purposes of the analyses on the movement to come, and their evaluations, we might state that clearly there can be political conse-

quences for works of literature. Still, Marinetti's desire
to change life is not so totally unique (remember Rimbaud)
and may not be said to run so nicely along the surface of
his rhetoric, but rather more surreptitiously at the mar-
gins: he wanted to change what he perceived to be a squalid
cultural consciousness with a good jolt.

The Futurist formula "art-action" which Marinetti intro-
duced in "War, the Only Hygiene of the World," embodies within its two parts the very fusion of art and reality. The
mission that the manifestos announced, and the arenas they
chose for agitation, beckoned with their liberation from
morality and logic in dangerously daring ways. They at-
tempted to prompt new recognition, to induce changes always
thinking they could achieve this behind the front-line of
a satisfactory, esthetic scope. The revolutionary reach of
"Uccidiamo il chiaro di luna" ("Let's Murder the Moonlight"),
the second Futurist Manifesto, also written in 1909, is
clearly checked by an artistic form not unlike Marinetti's
purely creative texts. It too is an elaborate prose poem
with many of the manners and themes which initially overflowed from the poems of the pre-Futurist period and in the
first manifesto:

> Let's break out of the horrible shell of
> wisdom and throw ourselves like fruit rip-
> ened with pride into the wide, crooked
> mouth of the wind! Let's give ourselves
> entirely to the Unknown, not in despera-
> tion but only to replenish the deep
> wells of the Absurd!

The 1913 manifesto "Destruction of Syntax--Wireless Imagina-
tion--Words in Freedom" announced "multiple and simultaneous
consciousness in a single individual" as a particular law
imposed by modernity. Futurist painter Umberto Boccioni
saw this as a new lyric expression, "the plastic manifesta-
tion of a new absolute: speed." The form corresponding to
the new fast rhythm of dynamic and simultaneous life, to
the civilization of "l'homme multiplié," passed from one
artistic medium to another. Words in freedom were formed
to correspond to Marinetti's own needs as it would become
the task of others to find their own form for unremitting
dynamism:

> I urged the Futurists to destroy and mock
> the garlands, the palms, the aureoles,
> the precious frames, mantles and stoles,
> the entire historical wardrobe and the
> romantic bric-a-brac that form a large
> part of all poetry before us. I proposed
> instead a fast, brutal and immediate
> lyricism, a lyricism that must seem anti-

> poetic to all our predecessors, a tele-
> graphic lyricism with no taste for ever
> being a book but, as much as possible,
> the taste of life...I initiate a typo-
> graphical revolution directed against
> the bestial and nauseating conception
> of the passéist and D'Annunzian book of
> verses, seventeenth century handmade pa-
> per, embellished with the helmets of
> Minerva and Apollo, zigzagging red in-
> itials, vegetables, mythological mis-
> sal ribbons, epigraphs and roman numer-
> als.

The "Technical Manifesto of Literature" had described in
1912 the "ridiculous" inability of syntax inherited from
Homer to deal with the world of the aviator. Words needed
to be freed from the "prison of the Latin sentence." The
first words in freedom Marinetti published, "Battle Weight
+ Stink," accompanied this manifesto. The following year
he provided spiralling aerial perspectives to make obsolete
traditional syntax and a mandate to ignore sentence struct-
ure.

Words in freedom, synoptic and freeword tableaux, and
aeropoetry all emanated from the model of the machine and
put into circulation the basic concepts of the Futurist and
Cubist vocabularies of dismemberment and dislocation. The
cinema inspired poets who sought to decompose and recompose
the movements of things without a subjective interference.
The 'I' and psychology were to be replaced by the material
itself. Theirs was a lyric obsession for things. Poems
with the guise of a poster or a musical score, complemented
by the telegraphically bombarding lines, then overlaid by
Marinetti's provocative and captivating oration, truly revealed their creator to be, as Ardengo Soffici remarked,
full of "sentiments, passions, enthusiam, instincts, intuitions."

The setting for Zang tumb tumb, Marinetti's great 'roman de montage,' was Hadrianopolis (Edirne, Turkey) during
a battle of the first Balkan War. The Balkan League in 1912
was composed of Bulgaria, Serbia, Greece and Montenegro.
After Turkey had declared war on Bulgaria, the Bulgarians
concentrated their forces in the Marizza Valley and staged
a siege of Hadrianopolis. Cholera broke out among the
Turks who then requested an armistice early in 1913. Oc-
cupation of the conquered territory provoked differences
among the League members and in August of 1913 Bulgaria at-
tacked Greece and Serbia, which were also supported by Rom-
ania and Turkey. Finally, the Bulgarians sought peace and
Hadrianopolis remained in Turkish hands.

Zang tumb tumb showcases a kind of literary terrorism, and extreme intransigence. Humanity at war is presented as the pinnacle of experience for Marinetti who was a correspondent at the front. These words in freedom glorify the spectacle before which they were created and whose inspiration unlocked different senses of plastic value. The battlefield as a Cubist playground, with aircraft and machine-gun parabolas, is regaled and reinvented for the page, where even calibrations, measurements and quantifications of the event taking place are mimicked: the degrees of the noise, the brightnesses of the light, the smell of the air, the altitude, the time, temperature, air-pressure are all recorded. The use of musical and mathematical signs also pay whimsical tribute to scientific exactitude. As a means of linguistic liberation and as symbols of Marinetti's new sensibility, words in freedom celebrate poetry's return to physical reality with full, vigorous, perhaps excessively calculated breaths. Like cinema, Zang tumb tumb seeks to surface out from poetry's shadows and re-establish contact with a new sensorial idealism. The result is a distant, static, relative of cinema syntax, endowing its representation of the physical world with movement and montage.

Marinetti's expressive poetic underwent many ground-rule revisions throughout the years, in an attempt to answer his critics and stall self-repetition. Freewordism expressed visual, olfactory and aural perceptions linguistically through free expressive orthography and onomatopoeia. He was especially good at creating the illusion of acceleration with pieces that seem related to automatic writing which Marinetti also claimed as his invention:

> Avant-garde heroism: 100 meters machine-
> guns shots eruption violins brass
> peem puum pac pac teem tuum machine-
> guns tataratatarata

> Avant-garde: 20 meters battalions-ants
> cavalry-spiders streets-fords general-
> islet dispatchers-grasshoppers sands-
> uprising howitzers-tribunes clouds-
> gratings guns-martyrs shrapnel-halos
> multiplication addition division
> howitzers-subtraction grenade-delet-
> ion streaming straining landslide
> blocks avalanche

The vitality of his humor counterbalances the machine-like rigidity which immediately vulgarizes the initially seductive Faustianism of technology. It is diluted by Marinetti's whimsical, optimistic energy. In his exaggerating what for us is an inhuman and ugly panorama, Marinetti translates

into text the great release of energy and confusion he has
witnessed, an explosion of movement beyond the ordinary a-
bility to register it.
In "The Technique of the New Poetry," written in 1937,
Marinetti continues to highlight the importance of speed
in his writing and introduces words in freedom of aeropoetry,
his latest variation:

> The simultaneous harmony invented by me
> is a retinue of limited essential synthetic
> verbalizations of diverse states of the soul,
> words in freedom, without punctuation, with
> infinitive verbs, adjective-atmosphere and
> strong contrast of verb tenses, which attain
> the highest aviational polyphonic dynamism
> still oratorical and comprehensible.

The earlier manifesto, "Geometrical and Mechanical
Splendor and Numerical Sensibility" explained how onomatopoeia, such as that found in "Dunes," could be indirect,
complex, analogical and abstract:

> Dum-dum-dum-dum expresses the circling sound
> of the African sun and its orange weight,
> creating a relation between sensations of
> weight, heat, color, smell and noise.

Such a notion, which serves as an alternative to the "ciel
antérieur où fleurit la beauté," breaks the reins of signifi-
cation and its tenuous mediation by installing what could
be viewed as one of the more esoteric and mysterious of
Marinetti's poetic statements. Abstract onomatopoeia does
not correspond to any natural sound, or any mechanical
sound, but instead expresses states of the soul.
In the art-prose of his "allegorical" novel Gli indomabili (The Untameables), ("Naked raw synthetic. Simultaneous
polychronographical polynoisemaking. Vast violent dynamic."),
Marinetti presents a gentler view of the human condition:
a reconciliation with nature and a version of transcendence.
The characters feature softer, less instinctual aggression.
The work's introduction repeats that

> words in freedom are a new way of seeing
> the universe, an essential valuation of
> it as the sum of forces in motion and
> intersecting at the conscious meeting-
> point of our creator 'I' and simultan-
> eously recorded with all the expressive
> means which are at our disposal. [4]

Many have written that Futurism's effectiveness as an avant-garde movement ebbed immediately after World War I. This is true in terms of its early, innocent call of action for its own sake. Marinetti continued to fashion a spiritual politics of action in his writing and there are many works by him which deserve attention as something other than examples of late Futurist writing.

By the time the autonomy of the movement had faded, Mussolini sought to establish an Italian Academy and the Futurist movement then took on the appearance of a school with a substantial number of young followers. It also contradicted its own founding principles by supporting nationalistic plans and handing their influence over for a niche in the official tradition. An editor's note, attached to the final pages in The First Aerial Dictionary, announced Marinetti's election to the Academy. There was disappointment that he had accepted this and Marinetti explained

> If I had not accepted the Academy, I would
> not have been able to launch you. Mussolini
> would not accept you and because he would not
> enter into Futurism, Futurism must establish
> itself in Fascism. It is Futurism which is
> entering the Academy and not the Academy
> which is entering Futurism. [5]

L'Aeropoema del golfo della Spezia (Aeropoem of La Spezia Gulf), published in 1935, was a patriotic book dedicated to the Gulf, the "synthesis of the forces and gentlenesses of Italy." Its introduction, entitled "Taking Off," also included the Manifesto of Aeropoetry which originally appeared in 1929:

> The characteristics of aviation that are
> the ascending rush the religion of speed
> the suspension without contact the indis-
> pensible health of the engine the dangers
> and sensibilities the fusion of man with
> the apparatus and the circling spherical
> perspective which has nothing to do with
> the horizon line of the ancient terres-
> trial poetry absolutely impose on Aero-
> poetry new means and principles.

One of these new principles was the attempt at a swifter, greater flow by fusing words together, "battagliafiume-pontebosco" ("battleriverbridgewood") for example. With a

desire to reduce the number of terrestrial images, Marinetti
applies geometric figures to the visual, auditory and tactile
sensations of flight where total command is also an important
factor.

Il poema non umano dei tecnicismi (The Non-Human Poem
of Technicisms) glorifies self-sufficient Italy. It is a
poem labelled inhuman by its author because it glorifies
technicisms "where the technical genius invades the spiritual realms" and rebels from nature.  In this text's introduction, "Systematic Extraction of New Splendors and New
Music of Technicisms," Marinetti asserts

> to reach an effectiveness the poetry of
> technicisms must, in the magnification of
> every single joy manifest the following
> qualities  1 anti-nostalgic optimism
> 2 anti-rhetorical simplicity  3 originality
> 4 variety  5 intensity  6 dynamism  7syn-
> thesis  8 typical tactilism  9 typical ol-
> factorism  10 typical uproarism.

Marinetti's life  ended during the war, at Bellagio,
Italy late in 1944 where, returning from voluntary service
in the Russian campaign, he wrote "Quarto d'ora di poesia
della X Mas" ("Quarter of an Hour of Poetry for the 10th
E-Boat Squadron").  Here, Marinetti's esthetic view of war
seems filled with a religious mood and the deep awareness
of Italy's fall.  Action, however, is once again praised:

> We will be we are the kneeling machine-guns
> with barrels trembling in prayer
>
> I kiss and kiss again the spiked weapons with
> a thousand thousand thousand hearts all pierced
> by the vehement eternal oblivion

As we read these poems today, we may find it a little
quaint to feel the excitement that the new technological
inventions of the beginning of the century produced in
Marinetti and the Futurists.  It may seem so surpassed, so
old-fashioned.  It may be better to equate this joy of living
at its most intense and frolicsome with the "happenings" of
the 60's, which owe something of their atmosphere to these
early modern counter-culture exponents.  Today, we can enjoy these writings as celebratory and, dare I say it, proto-
psychedelic.

Insofar as I have tried to convey the dynamics of
Marinetti's conceptualizations, I have passed along his ideas,
graphic, olfactory, onomatopoetic, tactile, and so on. In
these senses the Marinettian language is embedded quite
vividly in the matrix of culture, in the pastiche of all

signs. His collages of meaning contributed to the later realized works of many writers, as did Apollinaire's, and many of his curious literary twists resemble Gertrude Stein. Because of the numerous freeword principles outlined in the manifestos, and Marinetti's own bilingualism which prompted the publication of everything in French and Italian, his translator has many instances of assistance. To be able to see many poems in two languages to begin with provides a lot of help. I have tried to reproduce the contextual range and tonality of Marinetti's work in English with the hope of capturing for my own language something of those other languages' unrepeatabilities. Marinetti had intended that Futurism should reach all countries and led the way, even in translating himself (although Decio Cinti also helped). I think that much of the enjoyment and wonder which he intended to share has finally reached us.

I would like to thank those who read these pieces, felt some of the excitement they were meant to share, and offered insights and translation-help without which I could not have managed. I owe the most to my good friend Elizabeth A. Petroff who read the material probably as much as I did. Luigi Ballerini, Frank Fata, David Lenson, Don Eric Levine, Alessandra Robertazzi, and Frederic Will all offered invaluable assistance in translating, and I especially thank them.

I am also grateful for permission from Luciano De Maria and Arnoldo Mondadori Editore, Milan, to reproduce the original Italian pages of the frontispiece to Zang tumb tumb, and the poems "Correzione di bozze + desideri in velocità" and "Dune," from Teoria e invenzione futurista, edited by Luciano De Maria, 1986. I thank the journal OCTOBER and the MIT Press for permission to reproduce translations of "Corrections of Proofs + Desires in Speed" originally appearing in OCTOBER 24, published by the Massachusetts Institute of Technology Press, copyright 1983 by the Institute for Architecture and Urban Studies at MIT. Finally, I am grateful to Farrar, Straus and Giroux for permission to publish translations of works to which they own the original Italian rights.

R J P

Amherst

1986

14

[1] Robert Hughes, The Shock of the New (New York: Knopf, 1981) p. 40.

[2] F. T. Marinetti, ed. Enquête internationale sur le Vers Libre et manifeste du futurisme (Milan: Poesia, 1909) pp. 143-144.

[3] See Mario De Micheli, "Una prima 'teorizzazione' marinettiana" in La Matrice ideologico-letteraria dell'eversione fascista (Milan: Feltrinelli, 1975) pp. 9-24.

[4] For all of the manifestos quoted in this introduction, see F. T. Marinetti, Teoria e invenzione futurista, ed. Luciano De Maria (Milan: Mondadori, 1968).

[5] Patrizia Runfola, "Portrait synthétique de Marinetti" in Autoportrait et les amours futuristes par F. T. Marinetti ed. Gérard-Georges Lemaire (Paris: Centre Georges Pompidou, 1984) p. 169.

This introduction is indebted to the many enlightening observations and assertions to be found in the scholarly work published in Europe by the following critics: Par Bergman, Luciano De Maria, Mario De Micheli, Brunella Eruli, Ruggero Jacobbi, Giovanni Lista, Luigi Paglia and Bruno Romani. It is in such works that the most rewarding investigation of Futurism has been performed, and may they continue to have the formative influence for subsequent scholars, American and European, which they've had for me.

# AN EIFFEL TOWER OF WORDS

## I

Prematurely induced by intemperance of
knowledge, the old age of the world
drew on.  This the mass of mankind saw
not, or, living lustily although un-
happily, affected not to see. But, for
myself, the Earth's records had taught
me to look for widest ruin as the price
of highest civilization.

--Poe

## FANFARE OF THE WAVES

Ah! there you are, so unmasked, Stars!
Infamous courtesans with swollen and heavy
and translucent breasts
like two enormous drops of amber!
Divine go-betweens with eyes of pearl,
casters of evil spells and mortal charms!
.. .. .. .. .. .. .. .. .. .. .. .. ..
O sorceresses of the Impossible! Stars!
Promisers of nothing! There you are, before me
within reach of my vengeance! Oh my joy!
Oh! that I may savor the unbridled drunkenness
of spitting on your majestic faces!
Victory is certain, know it!
The victory is ours; we will be ten million
Waves at the assault of your metal walls!
.. .. .. .. .. .. .. .. .. .. .. .. ..
Stars, cursed forever, these are incandescent pyramids
of cadavers that the Cyclones lift and brandish
against you!
They are the petrified cadavers of your lovers,
dead from having drunk your poisoned kissing!
Yes, cursed! May your faces of love and bitterness,
Stars, your pupils full of the illusory looks
of our false mistresses be a thousand times cursed!

I will anoint your faces drenched in false tears
and made up with fleeting gentleness
with our greenish smoking spit!
Your adamant faces that once smiled
on my soul in the beautiful perverse evenings
of my youth, through the forests' hair
torturing a hot Spring anguish. . .
it is to tear your emerald faces
that I drag the armies of the sovereign Sea
along the steep slopes of an artificial mountain
to the assault of your dazzling turrets!
And my Waves are drunk with vengeance!
Beyond your inaccessible walls
we will chew your great golden hearts with a thousand
teeth! A hot carouse! and we will swallow them
into our humid and transparent bellies!
.. .. .. .. .. .. .. .. .. .. .. .. ..

from La Conquête des Étoiles, 1902

## PRAYER TO THE ALMIGHTY SEA

## TO DELIVER ME FROM THE IDEAL

Sea, divine sea, I don't believe,
will not believe, that the earth is round!
Our nearsighted senses!. . . Still-born syllogisms!...
Dead logics, Sea... I don't believe
you roll sadly over the world's back
like a viper on a stone!...
The Wise proclaim it, having measured all of you!...
They have sounded your waves! Who cares?...
They will never understand your delirious voice.

You are infinite and divine, I know
by the oath from your foaming lips,
repeated from beach to beach
by Echoes listening like spies,
by the oath silenced with thunder!...
Infinite and divine, you move along
like a great river, happy in its fullness.
Oh! who can sing the worthy epithalamium
of my soul swimming at your immense center?...
And the brilliant clouds signal to you
as you dive so simply, a straight line,
into the immeasurable depth of the horizon!...

Like river water reflecting gulps of fire,
yes, you plunge in a straight line!... and the Wise
are wrong, for I have seen you, at noons of deification,
risen against the Azure of aggravating betrayal!...
... For I have seen you red and cruel,
brandished inexorably
against the carnal side of a dying April eve,
amid the demonic hair of the Night!...
Sea, oh awesome sword about to split the Stars!...
Oh awesome sword
fallen from the broken hands of a dying Jehovah!...

And Sunsets, then transforming
are mere bloody wounds which you've delivered
through time, to avenge yourself, avenge yourself!...
What do the Wise say?
What do you say, old magic texts, eternal alembics,
silver scales, slanting telescopes?
But the Wise are wrong, whatever they say.
They are wrong for denying your holy nature,
because Dream exists and Science is nothing
but the sad faint of a Dream!...

You dive into the Infinite like an unremitting river
and the winding Stars of sapphire
lie cool upon your edges
in their metal, shimmering robes
with their unyielding folds!...
Meanwhile, imperious Stars
helmeted with fire, agile in their emerald girdles
hover over your shores, stretching their great arms
of light above the waves to bless you, oh Sea,
travelling in sky-blue prairies
expanding your eternal desire
and your voluptuous dementia,
oh radiant Veins of Space!...
Pure Blood of the Infinite!...

The Wise climbed atop your peaks,
to hang fidgetting like marionettes,
with strings tangled with the autumn rains,
to explore you, Oh Sea!...

They treat you like a poor slave,
toppled over and over, scourged upon the sand
by your hangmen, the Wind!...

They despise your sobs
and the flooding sadness in your eyes!...
They claimed that you surround the earth's curves
like the evil humors of our bodies,
--the dropsy of a dilapidated world!
Others have seen you green with bile and decay
and venom, reddening at twilight;
they add that you recoil, incessantly,
far from beaches, and you will die, sadly drained.
For them you are only an ancient golden snake,
twisted upon the hardened missals of the earth!...
Who cares?... the hammers and drills of your voice
will quickly crumble their fleeting words!...

I, who love you with all my despair stuck upon shore,
I, who believe in your holy power,
will sing of your triumphal course through space,
how you cross from shore to shore, unfolding
your sparkling, solemn waters
combed by squalls in the bosom of Infinity!...
Swell my soul like a golden sail!
Oh blood of the infinite, swell and finally submerge
the beach of my heart on this night of vertigo,
with your swollen tides of rays and purple!

Countless nostalgic Stars
have descended, Oh Sea,
into the majestic current of your river,
at swim, searching the wide horizon,
watching afar, carefully, into the distance for
the clear gold estuary of eternal coolness
to ease their hearts from their fiery knots
and the scalding of their arms of light!...

Oh Sea, Hurry! Hurry!... your giant, bullish
clouds, with monumental croups,
descend--see?...idly, toward your banks,
dragging the enormous chariots of the Constellations.
They've come to drink at your shining water,
waving their unshapely heads
under their divergent misty horns
and their nostrils trickling shining worlds!...

Heavens! How marvelous!... Loud echoes
reverberate the cry of amazement and bliss!...
The beautiful miracle, Oh Sea, is this finally it?...
Turbulent Sea, adventurous Sea!...
You are within me, as I desire you!...
Gallop on, in ecstasy with my liberated heart,
with the desperate pack of your baying tempests,
sounding the horn, emptying your lungs against the Stars,
beneath your romantic plume of disheveled clouds.

from <u>Destruction</u>, 1904

## SONG OF THE MENDICANT OF LOVE

to Isidore De Lara

I saw you one night a short while ago,
I don't know where, and then I waited, yearning...
Night, swollen with stars and blue perfumes
suspended her nakedness above me, dizzy
and shaken with love!...
Night madly opened her constellations
like palpitating, purple and gold veins,
and all the blood's illuminating pleasure
streamed into the vast sky...
I waited drunk beneath your glowing windows
alone blazing through the space.
I waited still for the supreme miracle
of your love, the ineffable charity
of your gaze...
...For I am a mendicant starved for the Ideal
walking along the shore
seeking love and kisses
to nourish my dream.
I defiantly lusted for the sky's jewels
to embellish your nakedness like a queen!...
And I held out my mad courtesy to you
like two gaunt and dying arms
bloodstained in the shadows!
And the fullness of my dream increased
everything!...
Bells rang in the sky, like monstrous
mouths... mouths of Destiny!...
The invisible, fierce bells seemed to open
above me like inverted abysses in the silence...

A high wall stood,
as high and implacable as despair!...
I waited alone, and thousands of stars,
mad stars, seemed to burst forth from your windows
like sparks flying out of a golden furnace!...
Your sweet shadow appeared at the hollow of the panes
like an infatuated soul, rolling
her suffering eyes
and you divine my delirious prey
up there, standing at the summit
of my Dream's sumptuous towers!...
My Love flourished its red rapiers
shining teeth and closed pupils,

with a great wave and rose wildly
toward your tragic splendor.

For I am the insatiate mendicant, walking
towards the palpitating warmth of your breasts
and the languor of your lips. . .
the implacable mendicant
who walks along the shore
imploring love and kisses
to nourish his dream!. . .

The dark night opened at the wall's base
and you appeared!. . .
. . . Everything was abolished
and my Dream shattered the world
with the beat of a wing!

Indeed, I think to myself
in the fabulous gardens
where my soul is exiled,
chimerical apple trees fashioned your winding flesh
by snowing their scented petals
in the sonorous fingers of the wind!. . .
I come to you, trembling and religious
as if in a temple. . .
groping at chance
as if in a humid grotto!. . .
I come to you, stumbling with my timid step
so as not to awaken Grief in passing!. . .
Your smile is revealed in the serene water
of your face, as if under the calm fall
of a flower.
Your smile unfurls in the wide sky
and makes the impetuous face
of the stars fade into silence!. . .
.. .. .. .. .. .. .. .. .. .. .. .. .. ..

. . . You asked me about my past,
my name and distant country,
all one usually asks
of exhausted travelers
drinking at the fountains. . .
.. .. .. .. .. .. .. .. .. .. .. .. .. ..

I followed you to your home.
We were alone, far from human crowds,
at the threshold of the Infinite

and I felt the softness of twilight
upon the sea, when one goes there
to the violet gulfs thoroughly damp
with silence.  We were alone
and my Dream sang to yours.
.. .. .. .. .. .. .. .. .. .. .. ..

from <u>Destruction</u>, 1904

## BABEL OF DREAMS

Sunsets with gold claws
beneath their manes of fire!...
Sunsets crouched at the horizon's edge
had torn my adolescent flesh
with their tawny paws outstretched
like lions!...

It was you, O crepuscular Sea, that gave me
a biting nausea for living and infinite sadness!...
Having contemplated you too much in my youth,
I now stagger in your breath, drunk with desperation!...

Some evenings down there, in bewitched Africa,
all of us, a mournful pack of schoolboys,
were guided over your morose beaches
dragging along sheeplike
under the custody of gloomy priests.
Silhouettes of ink that stained the intangible silk
of a beautiful Oriental sky!...

And you came indolently towards us, O sensual Sea,
fresh and green like a woman half naked
under the frills of foam, to dry
your snowy feet upon the sand...
Trembling with anger like a wild child,
you sulked at the lazy, lingering evening,
the beautiful evening, the lover rouging your cheeks!...
And you hurled our stars and dreams high above
as far as the zenith with the rolling
hollows and smoothnesses of your waves,
slack glass beads come to us from the Orient!...

My heart was drunk from the murmurings of pearls
that your weary hand shelled in the caves of the rocks!...
My heart sobbed between your burning fingers
like a Satanic lyre, whose stretched strings
exhausted by caresses, suddenly burst
with racking laughter!...
My heart? I rolled it in your nocturnal tresses...
My heart! I dragged it along, panting
beneath your foamy waves, toothed
like cruel silver saws!...

O contemptible Sea, a thousand times
disgraced according to astral laws,
you that peopled my pensive youth
with Levantine mouths open in spasmodic song,
and with the obscene twists of your sexy waves!...
O Oriental dancer with your heaving belly
and breasts red with the blood of shipwrecks!...

We walked
dragging our legs
like wounded dogs, with bloodstained ears
that quench their thirst in stagnant puddles...
already flowered with illusory stars!...
We dreamed aground, like mendicants
before the dazzling portal of the venerable night
where your frenetic fingers wrote the chronicles
of your shipwrecks in ebb and flow!...
And within my heart I held the sumptuous image
of a black palace with a hundred gold turrets
brandished against the sky, where the Bride
of Brides was finally imprisoned
and kept untouched,
conquered at the price of all the heavens
constellated in my dreams!...
And my eyes explored the bottom
of the hateful twilight
and the blue depth of fabulous grottos
among the green forks of clouds...

Later, when I returned home
a sweet, social family evening began
under the lamp lifting its neck of flame
to the sky, radiating its bright wings
upon the table and hatching my soul's
exalted desires in the flutter of its silky rays...
like a hen with large magic golden eggs
...in a dark corner
my wrinkled Sudanese nurse
sang sadly with her thin dark voice
marking the rhythm by clapping her hands
with a sound like castanets...
And in the suffocating evening
scorched by the heat,
the woman's voice colored the silence
with legends tangled like black heads,

broken up with white laughter
and crowned with scarlet feathers!...
I leaned out the window for a moment
O Sea, to hear you murmuring your entreaties
on the passing waves
like a streetwalker.

O Sea, who will come to share your violent bed
this evening... to caress the menacing turns
of your serpentine flesh...and bite
your breasts studded with fires
triggering against God in the tempests
until they bleed in a death-rattle?...

Suddenly, rising with a leap among the rocks,
frothy and savage
like a madman jumping in rage,
you shook your ivory arms
rattling your amulets
snapping your teeth
upon resounding pebbles...
.. .. .. .. .. .. .. .. .. .. .. .. .. .. ..

from Destruction, 1904

## MY SOUL IS A BRAT

to Her Serene Highness
Madame Princess of Monaco

O Sea, my soul is a brat
who squeals and struggles to have a plaything!...
Give him your heavy, big-bellied ships
moving with great pomp, carrying their masts
high, like priests with the poles
of shimmering, square banners
inflated with solar gold...
to amuse, O Sea, to amuse
my soul!

I savored you a thousand times
with all the hunger of my sturdy dream,
slack sails, half-lowered,
sails colored tan, rust and ochre,
sails more succulent than fabulous bunches
of grapes hanging from the rigging
like the scintillating vines in a Promised Land!...

Give me your violet and transparent grapes!
I beg you for my insatiate lips,
my soul's voracious eyes!

What a feast, what a radiant feast
to have you near me on calm summer evenings
with your serpent skin of chrysolite scales
and your rosy belly inlaid like a lizard's!...
Yahoo!
O Sea, I want to quench my thirst
in delight with the freshness
of your spray and the grains of frost
you leave on my lashes...
triumphal orgy of my senses!
I grip the lashing mane of your waves
and ride naked upon their vehement backs,
breathing with my open lungs
the acid and honeyed odor of a fleece
fermenting with blond putrefaction in the sun!...

I plunge with hands joined,
submerge, stroking with my arms
into the diaphanous softness
of your undulating breast
seekest the freshest blood
in your deep, green entrails...

The Sea has already absorbed
the vermilion blood of the evening,
all aglitter with silver particles
and now, slowly the gray sky curves
its vaults like funeral crypts
where lethargic Stars, still, suspended by a claw,
seem like strange bats with palmed gold wings!...

Sinisterly lined along the dark quays
enveloped by the thick mists of nightmare,
colossal Cranes transform themselves
into magical bronze kangaroos, turning
upon themselves. Their large pouches
are full of tiny shadows,
gesturing confusedly in the twilight,
in the smoke of their breath!...

The Sea in the distance, sumptuously dressed
with all the light fallen from the sky,
delicately changes into a magic desert
of waving golden sands
disappearing in the infinite.
Violet shadows ripple them
and a clever wind scales and engraves them
with gentle puffs,
with slow puerile fondling.

The colossal Cranes,
necks sinisterly outstretched,
watch for prey upon the sea!...
A steamer advances,
its prow headed directly towards me.
I watch it swell like an enormous ball
under its great masts flourished like lances!...
It approaches with long heavy steps,
moving its immense claws under the water
like a fantastic dromedary
half-immersed in water as it crosses
the rosy, placid ford
of a Paradisical Nile, irrigating
a vast meadow in the sky with gentle curves...

This changeable sea is only a mirage,
with chimerical sands of gold!

Now in the vague evening light
the strange dromedary grows larger,

darkening the bank with its shadow...
On the sides of its formidable hump
the immense pockets of a black sack swing slowly,
when I perceive copper-colored ears
pointed in confusion, in waiting,
directly at the Occidental horizon...
long fleecy backs of fabulous sheep
among the blackish caftans... and piles
of crates... and the long damascened rifles
of the Bedouins,
high as ships' masts
in the evening mist.

Suddenly the moon, white and juicy with light
bursting from the sky's middle like a fantastic coconut,
waves and rolls below
upon the dromedary's moving back.

Hooray! Hooray!... That, that fruit
can satiate me, the fruit
my soul has always called for
with its desert-traveler's burning thirst!...

I'm alone, upright
naked and dripping, standing upon a huge hill
of coke and, near me among dense clouds of nightmare,
the Cranes swoop slowly, scraping
the fearful depth of the horizon
with their necks of prophetic bronze.
Their crops, full of tinkling chains
suddenly throw off the white fear
of their long guttural and vaporous caw.
Then, like a spring
my heart leaps...

All my whetted nerves cry out
from the effluvia and tar
and from time to time become weakened
by the mixed freshness -- gilded honey
and black liquorice -- of rancid or musty fruits!...

Then, the wild and stimulating odor of sandalwood
hurls my heart again towards hate and dementia
drunk almost to death, leaping suddenly
in a circling dance like a feathered negro
crying in a red drunkenness
perforated by white laughter...

Higher, still higher
than the azure tears and sobs
with which the mourning bells
impregnate the hard landscape...
higher, still higher
than the tormented cries of boats
turned toward distant beaches...
higher, still higher
than the monotonous cough and exasperated sobs
from the steamers...
with all the resonant fullness
of my bronze lungs,
to your immense power, O gluttonous Sea,
I sing!
.. .. .. .. .. .. .. .. .. .. .. .. .. ..

from Destruction, 1904

## TO THE RUSSIAN REVOLUTIONARIES

You were so able, creeping around the tables
where the ribald and dead drunk generals
were wallowing, in halos of alcohol and the heat
of the candelabra,
...you were so very able, while pretending
to pick up some contemptible crumbs,
to steal under their napkins,
out from their pockets' bottoms
the key to their underground powder-boxes!...

And then?... And then, to run low like castor-oil,
salutary, into the stinking intestines
of the old palaces to throw there
the wounding golden fuse,
the crackling fuse that would deliver you!...

The crackling fuse that delivers you
from sinister patrols
with brazen measured steps in the silence...
from their dismal sabers' rattle
and handcuffs biting your wrists
while you dream your desires for freedom
asleep on the ramparts
in the memory of immensified moonlight!

The wounding fuse that delivers you
from sinister patrols whose laughing bayonets
suddenly sweep you beyond the walls,
pitilessly beyond the towns' thresholds
like some dirt!...

Some dirt?... So much the better!... Accumulate...
Accumulate, O living dirt!...
There we can hide the impatient dynamite.
It is a gay manner of fertilizing the earth!...
Because the earth, believe me,
will be pregnant, so pregnant... it will explode!...
from a lofty star,
into enlightening explosions!...

from La vita letteraria, III, 2
Rome, January 16, 1906

TO MY PEGASUS

Vehement God of a race of steel
Automobile drunk with space
trampling the bit in anguish between your strident teeth!
O formidable Japanese monster with forge-like eyes,
nourished with flames and oil,
starving for horizons and thunderstruck prey,
I unchain your diabolically beating heart
and your gigantic tires for the dance
that you lead over the white streets of the world.
Finally, I slacken your metallic reins...
You rush with ecstasy into the liberator Infinite!...
In the baying crash of your voice...
the setting sun encases your speedy step
accelerating its blood-red palpitation
flush with the horizon...
It gallops down below,
at the bottom of the woods... look!...

What does it matter, beautiful demon?...
I'm at your mercy... Take me!
Over the deaf earth, despite all its echoes,
beneath the blind sky, despite its gold stars
I go, aggravating my fever and desire...
And from time to time I straighten up
to feel the wind's cool and downy arms
wrap around my shuddering neck.

Your charming and distant arms attract me!
This wind is your engulfing breath,
O bottomless Infinite, absorbing my joy!...
Ah! Ah!...some black and lanky windmills
suddenly have the air to run
on their whalebone canvas wings
as if with immeasurable legs...
The mountains are preparing to hurl
mantles of somnolent freshness upon my flight...
There! There! Look! at this left turn!...
O monstrous livestock, Mountains, O mammoths
trotting heavily, bending your immense humps,
watch this... overtaken... drowned...
in the thick skein of fog!...
And I hear hazily
the purring din that tackles over the roads,
your colossal feet in boots seven leagues long...

Mountains with fresh cloaks of turquoise!...
Beautiful rivers breathing in the moonlight!...
Shadowy plains! I can overtake you
with a grand gallop on this enraged monster...
Stars, my Stars, do you hear its steps,
the baying crash and its metal lungs
collapsing interminably?

I accept the bet... with you, my Stars!...
Faster!... Faster still!...
Constantly, without a rest!...
Loosen the reins!... You can't?...
Then crush them!...
so the motor's pulse heaves a hundred times harder!

Hooray! No more contact with this dirty world!...
Finally I've lifted off and can fly
with suppleness upon the intoxicating fullness
of the Stars,
streaming
in the great celestial bed.

from La Ville charnelle, 1908

THE ART OF NOISE

II

One lingered long among the
dynamos, for they were new,
and they gave to history a
new phase.
                    --Adams

## LET'S MURDER THE MOONLIGHT

.. .. .. .. .. .. .. .. .. .. .. .. .. .. .. .. .. .. ..
In the deep night we were almost in the sky, upon the
high Persian plane, sublime altar of the world, whose immeasurable steps carry populous cities. Aligned to the infinite along the Railway Line, we panted over the melting
pots of barytes, of aluminum and manganese, that every so
often frightened the clouds with their dazzling explosion;
and watching over us in a circle, the majestic patrol of
the lions who, with tails erect, cast their manes to the
winds, and pierced the black, deep sky with their round
white roars.

But, little by little, the lucid, warm smile of the
Moon overflowed from the torn clouds, and when she finally
appeared, dripping with the inebriating milk of acacias,
the mad felt their hearts jump right out of their breasts
and climb to the surface of the liquid night.

All of a sudden a shrill cry cut the air, a noise so
omnipresent that everyone ran to it... It was a very young
madman, with virgin eyes, struck by lightning on the Rails.

His cadaver was immediately lifted. In his hand he
held a white and desiring flower, whose pistil stirred like
a woman's tongue. Some desired to touch but this was bad
because very quickly, with the facility of a dawn spreading
across the sea, a sobbing verdure rose by magic from the
earth rippled with sudden waves.

From the blue fluctuations of the meadow, there e-
merged the vaporous haloes of innumerable women swimming,
who opened sighing the petals of their mouths and damp
eyes. Then, in the intoxicating deluge of perfumes, we
saw grow a fabulous forest, continuously before us, whose
curving leaves seemed exhausted by a slow, slow breeze. A
bitter tenderness undulated... The nightingales drank the
fragrant shadows with long gurgles of pleasure and, from
time to time, they exploded into laughter within their cor-
ners playing hide-and-seek like quick and wicked children.
A soft, gentle sleep conquered slowly the forces of the
mad, who began to howl in terror.

The beasts impetuously rushed forward to assist them.
Three times, closed within bouncing skeins, with hooked
assaults of explosive rage, the tigers charged upon the
invisible phantoms in which the depths of that delightful
forest reboiled... Finally, a gap was opened: enormous con-
vulsions of wounded foliage, whose long moans woke the distant loquacious echoes hiding in the mountains. But while
we gave vent to our fury, all of us, to free our legs and

arms from the last tender lianas, we felt suddenly the carnal Moon, the Moon of beautiful warm thighs, abandoning
herself languidly upon our crushed backs.

A cry was heard in the airy solitude of the high
plains: --Let's murder the moonlight!

Some ran to nearby waterfalls; gigantic wheels were
raised and the turbines transformed the speed of water into magnetic spasms that rushed through the wires, up the
high poles, into the luminous, humming globes.

So it was that three hundred electric moons cancelled
the ancient green queen of loves with their blinding chalk
rays...

from Uccidiamo il chiaro di luna, 1909

BATTLE

(WEIGHT + STINK)

Midday 3/4 flutes moans dog-days tuumbtuumb alarms Gargar-
esch bursting crackling pus Tinkling knapsacks rifles clogs
nails cannon horses' manes wheels ammo wagons Jews grease-
marks oilcakes monotonous refrains discharges spurts lustre
bleariness stink cinnamon

must flux and reflux pepper brawl filth whirlwind orange
blossoms filigree misery nuts squares maps jasmine + nutmeg
+ rose arabesque mosaic carrion stings bungling

machine-guns = gravel + surf + frogs Tinkling knapsacks
rifles cannon scrap-iron atmosphere = lead + lava + 300
stenches + 50 fragrances pavement mattress detritus horse-
shit carrion fleec-flac crowding camels asses tuumb-tuuum
cesspool Souk-of-silver-mines labyrinth silk azure galabieh
purple orange-trees moucharabieh arches unhorsing branching
off little piazza swarming

tannery bootblack gandouras burnous swarming trickling
oozing polychromy confusion excrescences fissures holes
plaster debris demolition carbolic acid lime lice

Tinkling knapsacks tatatatata clogs nails cannon ammo
wagons lashings cloth from uniforms smell of lamb dead-end
on the left funnel on the right crossroads chiaroscuro
Turkish bath frying moss jonquils orange-blossom nausea
rose-essence deceit ammonia clutches excrement morsels
meat + 1,000 flies dried fruit carob chick-peas pistachios
almonds banana-regimen dates tuumbtuumb

fat goat moldy couscous aromas saffron tar rotten-egg wet-
dog jasmine mimosa sandalwood carnations maturing intensity
effervescence fermenting tuberose Putrifying scattering
fury dying breaking-up pieces crumbs dust heroism worms

tatatata rifle-fire peec pac puun pan pan mandarin tawny
wool machine-guns rattles leper's hovels sores forward

clammy meat filthiness gentleness ether Tinkling knapsacks
rifles cannon ammo wagons wheels gum-resin tobacco incense

anise village ruins burnt amber jasmine houses guttings
abandoned terra-cotta gutter tuumbtuumb violets shadows
wells donkey ass cadavers smash sex show

garlic bromine anise breeze fish spruce-new rosemary deli-
catessens palmtrees sand cinammon Sun gold balance plates
lead sky silk heat stuffing purple azure scorching Sun =
volcano + 3,000 banners atmosphere precision bullfight
rage surgery lamp

rays Bistouries sparkling cotton materials desert clinic x
20,000 arms 20,000 legs 10,000 eyes rifle-sights scintill-
ations awaiting operations sands ship-furnaces Italians
Arabs 4,000 meters battalions-boilers commands-pistons
sweat mouths furnaces

god's sake ahead oil tatatata ammonia  acacias violets
turds roses sands shaving-mirrors all walking arithmetic
traces obeying irony enthusiasm

droning stitching dunes pillows zigzags mending feet mill-
stones grinding sand the uselessness machine-guns = gravel
+ surf + frogs

Avant-garde:  200 meters fixed bayonets ahead Arteries
swelling hot fermentations hair armpits wood billets tawni-
ness blondness breezes + backpack 18 kilos prudence = see-
saw scrap-iron money-box softness: 3 shudders commands
stones rage enemy disaster lightness glory

Avant-garde heroism:  100 meters machine-guns shots
eruption violins brass peem puum pac pac teem tuum
machine-guns  tataratatarata

Avant-garde:  20 meters battalions-ants cavalry-spiders
streets-fords general-islet dispatchers-grasshoppers sands-
uprising howitzers-tribunes clouds-gratings guns-martyrs
shrapnel-halos multiplication addition division howitzers-
subtraction grenade-deletion streaming straining landslide
blocks avalanche

Avant-garde:  3 meters melanging coming and going on
shoulders coming off wounding fire uprooting dockyards
landslide fire panic blinding crushing entering leaving
running

Mud-splash Lives-rockets hearts-delicacies bayonets-table-
forks gnawing carving stinking dancing leaping fury trig-
gers-explosion howitzers-gymnasts clashes-trapezes

explosion rose joy bellies-watering-cans heads-footballs
dispersal Cannon 149-elephants artillery-cornacs heave-ho
anger levers slowness heaviness hub jockey method monotony
trainers range grand-prize parabola X light zang-tuumb-
tuuum hammer infinite Sea + lace-emeralds-coolness-elas-
ticity-abandonment-softness warships-steel-conciseness-
order Banner-of-combat (meadows sky-white-with-hot blood)
= Italy power Italian-pride brothers wives mother insomnia
cry-of-news glory domination coffee war-stories

Turrets cannon-virility-chase erection range-finder ecstasy
tuumb-tuumb 3 seconds tuumbtuumb waves smiles laughter ceec
chiac plaff pluuff gluugluugluugluu playing-hide and seek
crystal undefiled meat jewels pearls iodine salt bromide
little skirts gas liquor bubbles 3 seconds

tuumb-tuumb official whitening range-finder cross fire ring-
ring loudspeaker sight-4-thousand-meters hard to left good
all-steady dispersal-7-grades erection splendor flash
piercing immensity azure feminine deflowering

Rabidness corridors shriek labyrinth mattresses sobs breaking through desert bed precision range-finder monoplane
upper gallery applause

monoplane = balcony-rose-wheel-drum drill gadfly  arab-
defeat ox bloodiness massacre wounds refuge oasis humidity
fan freshness

siesta creeping germination effort vegetable-expansion
I'll-be-greener-tomorrow let's-keep-wet Serbian this-drop-
of-water need-to-climb-3-centimeters-to-resist-to-20-grams-
of-sand-and-3,000-grams-of-darkness milky-way-coco-palm
coconut-stars milk dripping sugar delight

from I poeti futuristi, 1912

## THE DUOMO OF MILAN

O Duomo of Milan, I have terrified you,
skimming your monstrous steeples
of centuried cliffs
with my gull's wings.
You say I am a Milanese who moves too fast.
In fact your dismayed tenderness
stains yellow and red
and black and green and white
the transparent skin
of your chameleon-like glass windows.
I irritate you every evening
flinging the ball of my heart
higher than your little golden madonna.

O Duomo of Milan
O boundless octopus with white tentacles,
you tremble when you feel
the immense net of flashing rails
wrap around you with all their streetcars,
multi-colored rings
adorning the evening
with green seaweed and coral.
Are you weeping at your fate,
cathedral stranded in the middle
of the noisy tumult
from the greatest train station in the world?
The day will come
(the Milanese are capable of it)
when they will build a colossal train
drawn by a giant locomotive
to carry you back into Paradise
from where you were sent in other times
by the Gondrand Brothers!

from Le Monoplan du Pape, 1912

## DESTRUCTION OF SYNTAX--WIRELESS IMAGINATION--
## WORDS IN FREEDOM

The Futurist Sensibility.
My Technical Manifesto of Futurist Literature (May 11, 1912) in which I invented "essential and synthetic lyricism, wireless imagination and words in freedom," concerns poetic inspiration exclusively.

Philosophy, the exact sciences, politics, journalism, education, business, must still make use of syntax and punctuation, however much they research synthetic forms of expression. In fact, I am constrained to use them myself in order to explain my ideas to you.

Futurism is based upon the complete renewal of human sensibility brought about by the effect of great scientific discoveries. Those who use the telephone today, the telegraph, the phonograph, the train, bicycle or automobile, the ocean liner, dirigible or airplane, the cinema or a great daily newspaper (the synthesis of a day in the whole world) do not dream that these diverse forms of communication, transportation and information exert such a decisive influence upon their psyches.

An ordinary man can travel in a day by train from his dead little village of deserted piazzas where the sun, dust and the wind silently play, to a great capital bristling with lights, action and sound. The inhabitant of an Alpine village can tremble with anguish every day with his newspaper, following the rebelling Chinese, London and New York suffragettes, Doctor Carrel, and the sleds of heroic polar explorers. The cowardly, sedentary inhabitant of some provincial town can permit himself the intoxication of danger by following the spectacle on film of a great hunting party in the Congo. He can admire Japanese athletes, black boxers, inexhaustible American eccentrics, the most elegant Parisian ladies, just by paying a franc on variety theater. Then, tucked into his bourgeois bed, he can enjoy the distant, expensive voice of a Caruso or a Burzio.

These now commonplace possibilities arouse no curiosity in superficial minds absolutely unable to grasp some new fact like "the Arabs who watched with indifference the first airplanes in the skies over Tripoli." However, for a sharp observer these things are important modifiers of our sensibility, causing the following significant phenomena:
1. Acceleration of life to today's rapid rhythm. Physical, intellectual and sentimental balance upon a tightrope of speed stretched between contrary attractions. Multiple, simultaneous consciousness in a single individual.

2. Horror of the old and known. Love for the new and unexpected.
3. Horror of calm living, love of danger and an aptitude
for daily heroism.
4. Destruction of the sense of a Beyond and an increased
value for the individual who wants "vivre sa vie" in
Bonnot's words.
5. Multiplication of human desire and ambition, breaking
breaking down all barriers.
6. An exact awareness of what is out of reach and unreal-
izable in every person.
7. Near-perfect equality between men and women and in their
social rights.
8. Depreciation of 'amore' (sentimentality or lust) produced by the greater freedom and erotic facility of women
and by the universal exaggeration of feminine luxury. Let
me explain: today women love luxury more than love. A trip
to a great dress-maker accompanied by some paunchy, gouty
banker friend who will pay, replaces perfectly the hottest
assignation with a young lover. The woman finds all the
mystery of love in selecting an unusual toilette, the latest model which her friends haven't yet gotten. Men hard-
ly love women lacking in luxury. The lover has lost all
his prestige and Love has lost its absolute value. A complex question which I must be content to skim over.
9. A modification of patriotism, nowadays become the heroic idealization of the commercial, industrial and artistic
solidarity of a people.
10. A modification in the conception of war, which has become the necessary and bloody test of a people's power.
11. The passion, art and idealism of Business. A new financial sensibility.
12. Man multiplied by the machine. A new mechanical sense,
a fusion of instinct with the efficiency of an engine and
conquered force.
13. The passion, art and idealism of Sports. Idea and love
of the 'record.'
14. New touristic sensibility of ocean liners and grand
hotels (the annual synthesis of many races). Passion for
the city. Negation of distances and nostalgic haunts.
Derision for "divine green silence" and intangible land-
scapes.
15. The earth made smaller by speed. A new sense of the
world. Let me explain: men have successfully conquered
the sense of home, the sense of a neighborhood, the sense
of a city, of a geographic area, of a continent. Today
they have a sense of the entire world. They little need to
know what their grandfathers did, but they must know what
their contemporaries from every part of the world are do-
ing. So it is necessary for every individual to communic-

ate with all people. A consequent need of feeling oneself
to be the center, judge and engine of the explored and un-
explored infinite. Enormous growth of a sense of humanness
and an urgent need to fix our rapport with all mankind at
every moment.
16. Disgust for curved lines, spirals and 'tourniquets.'
Love for the straight line, the tunnel. The practice of
visual foreshortening and synthesis created by the speed-
ing trains and automobiles looking down upon cities and the
countryside. Horror of slowness, trifles, analyses and
minute explanations. Love of speed, abbreviation and sum-
mary. "Quickly tell me everything in two words!"
17. Love for profundity and essence in every exercise of
the spirit.
Here then are some of the elements of the new Futurist
sensibility which has generated our pictorial dynamism, our
ungentle music of irregular rhythm, our art of noise and
our words in freedom.

Words in Freedom.
Rejecting every stupid definition and all the confused ut-
terances of professors, I now declare that lyricism is the
rarest faculty of intoxicating yourself with life, filling
life with your own intoxication. The faculty of changing
the turbid water of life flowing and covering us into wine.
The faculty of coloring the world with the very special
colors of our changeable 'I.'
Suppose a friend of yours endowed with this lyric faculty found himself in an area of intense life (revolution,
war, shipwreck, earthquake, etc.) and came immediately to
give you his impressions. Do you know what your lyric and
affected friend would do instinctively?
He would begin by brutally destroying the syntax of his
speech. He wouldn't waste time constructing sentences.
In his haste he wouldn't care about his punctuation and adjectives. He would throw off frenetically from his nerves
visual, auditory and olfactory sensations according to their
necessary flow. The rush of steam-emotion would burst the
sentence's pipeline, the valves of punctuation and adjecti-
val clamps. Handfuls of essential words with no convention-
al order. The narrator's only preoccupation is to render
all the vibrations of his 'I.'
Moreover, if this gifted lyrical narrator's mind was rich
in general ideas, his feelings would involuntarily inter-
twine with the whole universe known or intuited by him. And
in order to give exact value and proportion to his lived
life, he would cast immense nets of analogies over the world.
In this way he would telegraphically transmit the analogical
foundation of life with the same economical speed that a
telegraph imposes on the swift accounts of reporters and war-

correspondents. This need for the laconic applies not only to the laws of speed which govern us but also to the centuries-old rapport between audiences and poets. There runs the same bond which exists between two friends. They understand each other with only half a word, a gesture, a wink. So the poet's imagination must weave together distant things 'with no connecting wires' by means of essential words 'in freedom.'

The Death of Free Verse.
After having had a thousand reasons for existing, free verse is now destined to be replaced by words in freedom.
    The evolution of poetry and human sensibility has shown two irremediable defects in free verse.
1. Free verse pushes the poet fatally towards facile sound effects, a banal playing with speech, monotonous cadences, foolish rhymes and the inevitable reply of internal and external echoes.
2. Free verse channels artificially the flow of lyric emotion between the high walls of syntax and the dams of grammar. Free intuitive inspiration which directly addresses the intuition of the ideal reader is imprisoned and distributed like drinking water for the quenching of all restless and meticulous intelligences.
    When I speak of destroying the canals of syntax, I am being neither categorical nor systematic. Traces of regular syntax and even some very logical sentences can be found here and there in my words in freedom of unchained lyricism. This inequality in concision and freedom is natural and inevitable; poetry being in reality only a superior, more concentrated and intense life than that which we live every day, and, like the latter, composed of ultra-living and dying elements.
    Therefore there is no need to be preoccupied with this. But we should at all costs avoid rhetoric and banalities expressed telegraphically.

The Wireless Imagination.
By wireless imagination I mean the absolute freedom of images or analogies, expressed by disconnected words and with no wire conductors of syntax and no punctuation.
            Writers have finally abandoned themselves
            to immediate analogy. For example, they
            have compared an animal with a man or with
            another animal, which is almost like photo-
            graphy. They have compared a fox terrier
            to a tiny thoroughbred. Others, more ad-
            vanced, might compare that same trembling
            fox terrier to a little Morse Code machine.
            I compare it to boiling water. In this
            there is an 'ever wider gradation of anal-

ogies,' there are ever deeper, more solid
rapports, however distant.  Analogy is nothing more than a deep love that ties dis-
tant-seeming, different, even hostile
things.  An orchestral style, polychroma-
tic, polyphonic and polymorphous all at
once, embraces the life of the material
only by means of very vast analogies.
     When, in my "Battle of Tripoli" I
compared a trench bristling with bayonets to an orchestra, a machine-gun to
a 'femme fatale,' I intuitively intro-
duced a large part of the universe into
a brief episode of African battle.  Images
are not flowers to pick and choose stin-
gily, as Voltaire said.  They are the very
blood of poetry and poetry should be an
uninterrupted flow of new images, without
which there would be mere anemia and
chlorosis.  The wider their rapports, the
longer the images will maintain their power to astound. (Technical Manifesto)
The wireless imagination and words in freedom will carry
us to the essence of our material.  In discovering new
analogies between distant and apparently opposed things,
we will always value them as more intimate.  Instead of
'humanizing' animals, vegetables and minerals (a surpassed
system) we will be able to 'animalize, vegetize, mineralize,
electrify the style,' by making it live with the life of
its material.  For example, to give life to a blade of
grass I could say, "Tomorrow I'll be greener."  With words
in freedom we will have:  Condensed Metaphors--Telegraphic
Images--The Sum of Vibrations--Nodes of Thought--Balances
of Color--Open or Closed Fans of Movement--The Ends of
Analogies--Dimensions, Weights, Measures and the Speed of
Sensations--The Dive of the Essential Word into the Water
of Sensibility, without the Concentric Circles Produced by
the Word--Reposes of Intuition--Movements in Two, Three,
Four, Five Beats--The Analytic, Exploratory Poles that
Sustain a Group of Intuitive Wires.


Death of the Literary I.
Molecular Life and Material.
My Technical Manifesto fought the obsessive 'I' which poets
have described, sung, analyzed and vomited up to this day.
To get rid of it, we must abandon the habit of humanizing
nature by attributing human passions and preoccupations to
animals, plants, water, stones and clouds.  Instead we must
express the infinitely tiny all around us, the imperceptible,
the invisible, the agitation of atoms, the Brownian movements, all the passionate hypotheses and dominating ex-

plorations of high-powered microscopes. Let me explain:
I want to introduce infinite molecular life into poetry
not as a scientific document but as an intuitive element
that must mix with a work of art the infinitely great spec-
tacles and drama because such a fusion constitutes the in-
tegral synthesis of life.

To assist the intuition of the ideal reader I will use
italics for the words in freedom which will express infinitely small, molecular life.

The Semaphoric Adjective.
The Lighthouse Adjective or Atmosphere Adjective.
Everywhere we tend to suppress the qualifying adjective because it presupposes an arrest in intuition, too minute a
definition of the noun. This is not categorical. It is a
question of a tendency. We must make use of the adjective
as little as possible and in a way that is different. It
is necessary to think of them as railway signals or semaphoric signals of style regulating impulses, stalls and
stops of the race, of the analogies. As many as twenty
semaphoric adjectives may accumulate.

I call the adjective separated from nouns, isolated in
parentheses, a semaphoric adjective. And so the nouns become a kind of absolute, vaster and stronger than ordinary
nouns.

The semaphoric or lighthouse adjective, suspended from
its glass-framed cell of parentheses, throws its turning
beam far out and around.

The profile of this adjective unravels, overflows, illuminating, impregnating and enveloping a whole area of
words in freedom. For example, if in an agglomerate of
words in freedom used to describe a sea-voyage I place the
following semaphoric adjectives between parentheses:
(CALM, BLUE, METHODICAL, HABITUAL) not only the sea is
'calm, blue, methodical, habitual,' but the ship, its engines, the passengers, all that I create with my own spirit
are 'calm, blue, methodical, habitual.'

The Infinitive.
Here too, my declarations are not so categorical. I maintain however, that in a violent and dynamic lyricism the
infinitive verb will be indispensible. Round as a wheel,
adaptable like a wheel to all the cars of the train of
analogies, it constitutes the very speed of style.

In itself, the infinitive denies the existence of the
sentence and prevents style from slowing and stopping at
a certain point. While the infinitive is round and fluent
like a wheel, the other moods and tenses of the verb are
either triangular, square or oval.

Onomatopoeia and Mathematical Symbols.
When I said that it was necessary to spit every day upon the
Altar of Art, I incited Futurists to free lyricism from the
solemn atmosphere of uneasiness and incense where one calls
Art with a capital A. This Art constitutes the clerical
spirit. I urged the Futurists to destroy and mock the garlands, the palms, the aureoles, the precious frames, mantles
and stoles, the entire historical wardrobe and romantic bric-
a-brac that form a large part of all poetry before us. I
proposed instead a fast, brutal and immediate lyricism, a
lyricism that must seem anti-poetic to all our predecessors,
a telegraphic lyricism with no taste for ever becoming a
book but, as much as possible, the taste of life. Beyond
that the courageous introduction of onomatopoetic harmonies
to render all the sounds and noises of modern life, even
the most cacophonic.
     Onomatopoeia which vivifies lyricism with crude, brutal
elements, was used in poetry (from Aristophanes to Pascoli)
timidly, more or less. We Futurists initiate the continual
and audacious use of onomatopoeia. This must not be systematic. For instance, my "Hadrianopolis Siege-Orchestra"
and my "Battle Weight + Stink" required many onomatopoetic
harmonies. With the aim of giving the largest number of
vibrations and a deeper synthesis of life, we abolish all
stylistic bonds, all the bright clasps with which traditional poets linked their images in their versifying. Instead,
we advocate the use of very brief, anonymous mathematical
and musical symbols; we put between parentheses indications
like (presto), (più presto), (rallentando), (due tempi) to
regulate the speed of style. These parentheses can even
cut into a word or an onomatopoetic harmony.

The Typographical Revolution.
I initiate a typographical revolution directed against the
bestial and nauseating conception of the passéist and
D'Annunzian book of verses, the seventeenth century hand-
made paper embellished with helmets, Minervas and Apollos,
zig-zagging red initials, vegetables, mythological missal
ribbons, epigraphs and roman numerals. The book must be
the Futurist expression of our Futrist thought. Not only
that. My revolution is directed against the so-called
typographical harmony of the page, which is contrary to
flux and reflux, the starts and bursts of style running
through the page. Therefore, on a single page we could use
three or four colors of ink, and even twenty different type-
faces if necessary. For example, italics for a series of
similar or swift sensations, round heavy type for violent
onomatopoeia, etc. With this typographical revolution and
multi-color variety of characters I mean to redouble the
expressive force of words.
     I fight the decorative and precious esthetic of Mallarmé

and his search for the exceptional word, the one indispensable, elegant, suggestive, exquisite adjective. I don't
want to suggest an idea or a sensation with passeist grace
and affectation. I want rather to seize them brutally and
toss them in the reader's face.

I also combat the static ideal of Mallarmé with the
typographical revolution which allows me to impress on words
(already free, dynamic, torpedo-like) all the speeds of the
stars, the clouds, airplanes, trains, waves, explosives,
globules of sea-foam, molecules and atoms.

In this manner I realize the fourth principle of my First
Futurist Manifesto (Feb. 20, 1909): "We affirm that the beauty of the world grows richer with a new beauty: the beauty
of speed."

Multilinear Lyricism.
I have also devised multilinear lyricism with which I have
succeeded in reaching that lyric simultaneity which also
fascinates Futurist painters: multilinear lyricism by means
of which I am convinced the most complex lyric simultaneities
are obtained.

On several parallel lines, the poet will throw several
chains of color, sound, noise, weight, depth, analogy. One
of these lines could be olfactory, for example, another musical, another pictorial.

Let us suppose that the chain of pictorial sensations
and analogies dominates the other chains of sensations and
analogies: in this case they will be printed in a heavier
typeface than the second and third lines (for example, one
containing the chain of musical sensations and analogies,
the other the chain of olfactory sensations and analogies).

Given a page containing many groups of sensations and
analogies, each of which is composed of three or four lines,
the chain of pictorial sensations and analogies (in boldface)
will form the first line of the first group and continue on
the first line of all the other groups.

The chain of musical sensations and analogies (second
line), less important than the chain of the pictorial (first
line) but more important than the olfactory chain (third line)
will be printed in a smaller type than the first line and
larger than the third line.

Free Expressive Orthography.
The historical necessity of free expressive orthography was
demonstrated by the successive revolutions that have always
freed the lyric power of the human race from fetters and rules
1. In fact, poets began by directing their lyric intoxication into a series of equal breaths, with accents, echoes,
assonances or pre-established rhymes at a fixed interval
(traditional metric). Then they varied these different
measured' breaths with a certain freedom.

2. Later poets realized that the different moments of their lyric intoxication were able to be created with breaths adequate for the most diverse and unforseen intervals, with absolute freedom of accentuation. Thus they arrived at 'free verse,' but they still held on to the syntactical order of words, until lyric intoxication was able to filter down to the spirit of the listener through the logical canal of syntax.

3. Today we no longer wish lyric intoxication to order the words syntactically before throwing them out in breaths, and we have 'words in freedom.' Moreover, our lyric intoxication must freely deform, reshape words, cut them, stretch them, reinforce their centers or their extremities, augment or diminish the number of their vowels and consonants. Thus we will have 'new orthography' which I call 'free expressive.' This instinctive deformation of words corresponds to our natural tendency toward onomatopoeia. It matters little if the deformed word becomes ambiguous. It will marry to the onomatopoetic harmonies, or the summaries of noises, and soon will permit us to reach the 'onomatopoetic psychic' harmony, the sonorous but abstract expression of an emotion or pure thought. You may object that my words in freedom, my wireless imagination, demand special declamations, under pain of not being understood. Although I could care less about the comprehension of the many, I will respond that the number of Futurist speakers is multiplying, and that any admired traditional poem demands a special orator in order to be tasted for that matter.

May 11, 1913
published in <u>Lacerba</u> June 15, 1913

# F. T. MARINETTI
**FUTURISTA**

# ZANG TUMB TUUUM

## ADRIANOPOLI    OTTOBRE 1912

## PAROLE IN LIBERTÀ

EDIZIONI FUTURISTE

DI "POESIA,,

**Corso Venezia, 61 - MILANO**

**1914**

# Correzione
# di bozze + desideri
# in velocità

Nessuna poesia prima di noi
colla nostra immaginazione senza fili parole
in libertà vivaaaaAAA il FUTURISMO finalmente finalmente finalmente finalmente
finalmente

# FINALMENTE

ᴘᴏᴇSIA NASCERE

treno    treno    treno    treno    **tren  tron**
**tron  tron** (ponte  di  ferro:  **tatatluuun-**
**tlin)  sssssslll    sslissli    sslisssslll**
treno    treno    febbre    del    mio

Reproduced with permission from Luciano De Maria, editor,
Teoria e invenzione futurista, Milan: Arnoldo Mondadori
Editore, 1986.

# Correction
## of proofs + desires
### in speed

No poetry before ours
with   our   wireless   imagination   words
in freedom longggGGG live FUTURISM fi-
nally         finally         finally         finally
finally

## FINALLY

POETRY BEING **BORN**

train    train    train    train    **tren   tron**
**tron**    **tron**    (iron    bridge:    **tatluuuun-**
**tlin)**    **sssssssiii**    **ssiissii**    **ssiisssssiiii**
train    train    fever    of    my

treno express-express-expressssssss press-press
press - press - press - press - press - press - press - press -
press-press-presssssssss punzecchiato dal sale
marino aromatizzato dagli aranci cercare mare
mare mare balzare balzare rotaie rott-
tttaie balzare rooooottttaie roooooooottaie
*(GOLOSO SALATO PURPUREO FALOTICO INE-*
*VITABILE INCLINATO IMPONDERABILE FRA-*
*GILE DANZANTE CALAMITATO)* spiegherò
queste parole voglio dire che cielo mare
montagne sono golosi salati purpurei ecc.
e che io sono goloso salato purpureo ecc.
tutto ciò fuori di me ma **anche in
me** totalità simultaneità sintesi assoluta =
superiorità della mia poesia su tutte le
altre stop                    Villa San Giovanni
          cattura + pesca -+- ingoiamento
del treno-pescecane immagliarlo spingerlo nel

train express-express-expresssssssss press-press press-press-press-press-press-press-press-press-press-press-presssssssss stung by the sea salt aromatized by the oranges seeking the sea sea sea jumping jumping rails rails jumping rrrrrails rrrrrails *(GREEDY SALTY PURPLE FANTASTIC IN-EVITABLE SLOPING IMPONDERABLE FRA-GILE DANCING MAGNETIC)* I will explain these words I mean the sky sea mountains are greedy salty purple etc. and that I am greedy salty purple etc. all that outside me as well **as in me** absolute totality simultaneity synthesis = the superiority of my poetry over all others stop Villa San Giovanni capture + fish + enjoyment of the train-shark netting it pushing it

ferry-boat-balena                    partenza   della
stazione   galleggiante                        solidità
del   mare   di   quercia   piallata
                indaco                          venti-
lazione *(INSENSIBILE QUOTIDIANO METODICO*
*SERICO IMBOTTITO METALLICO TREPIDANTE*
*RITAGLIATO IMPACCHETTATO CESELLATO*
*NUOVO)*                accensione   di   un   veliero $=$ lampada   a   petrolio $+$ 12   para-
lumi   bianchi $+$ tappeto   verde $+$ cerchio
di   solitudine   serenità   famiglia
metodo   d'un   secondo   veliero   prua   lavorare
al   tornio   il   metallo   del   mare
trucioli   di   schiuma   abbassarsi   della   tempera-
tura $=$ 3   ventagli   al   disopra   dei   Monti
Calabri   *(AZZZZZZURRRRRRO LENTO INDUL-*
*GENTE SCETTICO)*
Macerie   di   Messina   nello   stretto

in the ferry-boat-whale          departure of

the floating station                    solidity

of the planed oaken sea

            indigo                          ventila-

tion *(INSENSIBLE DAILY ORDERLY METHODICAL*

*SILKY    STUFFED    METALLIC    TREMBLING*

*CUT-OFF    PACKED    UP    POLISHED*

*NEW)*                          ignition of a sailing

ship  **=**  a kerosene lamp  **+**  12 white

lampshades  **+**  a green carpet  **+**  circle

of solitude serenity family

method of a second ship prow working

the metal of the sea at its lathe

foam shavings being lowered by the

temperature  **=**  3 fans above the mountains

of Calabria *(AZZZZZZURRRRRRE SLOW INDUL-*

*GENT SKEPTICAL)*

Debris of Messina in the straits

terremoto di muraglie-fango            sen-
tire il mare come una somma di pesi
diversi            navigare = addizione
200.000 blocchi travi funi barili **(pluuuum)**
**+** milione sacchi bleu soffitti fradici porte
verdi carrozzelle gialle **+** 2.000 gravidanze
a vapore        **tataplumplum flac
flac** contro la prua-ventre        tenere
in bocca  tutto mare TONDO = nuota-
tore giocoliere **+** piatto porcellana (6 Km.
diametro) fra denti

# LUNA *(GIALLO VECCHIO)*

**a**

**picco**
sussulti bianchezza ronzii nascita esasperazione

earthquake of walls-mud　　　　　　feeling the sea as a sum of different
weights　　　　　navigating = addition
200,000 blocks beams ropes barrels
**(ploooom)** + a million sacks blue rotten
ceilings green doors yellow cabs
+ 2,000 steam pregnancies **tataploom-**
**ploom flac flac** against the prow-
stomach　　　　holding in its mouth the
entire ROUND SEA = swimmer juggler
+ porcelain dish (6 Km. in diameter)
between the teeth

# MOON *(OLD YELLOW)*

## over

## head

tremors whiteness buzzings birth exaspera-

di **4** globi elettrici sospesi sul treno fermo
in stazione galleggiante del ferry-boat

# LUNA *(LATTE SPORCO)*

**a**

## picco

luce sufficiente correggere bozze del mio
libro su Adrianopoli
no no nausea                    presenza
della città assediata nello stretto voltare le
spalle a Messina-Mustafà-Pascià
affastellamento graduato di Villa · San Giovanni ruzzolare di **8** lampade elettriche
nel mare                    a destra **2ª** cascata
di fuochi bianchi Reggio                    sotto

tion of 4 electric lights hanging on the
train stopped in the floating station of
the ferry-boat

# MOON *(DIRTY MILK)*

## over

## head

light sufficient for correcting the galley
proofs to my book on Adrianople
no no nausea                             appearance
of the besieged city in the straits turning away
from Messina-Mustafa-Pascia
the       graduated      heap      of      Villa
San   Giovanni   tumbling   of   8   electric
lights into the sea            to the right Reggio
2nd cascade of white fire                 beneath

miei piedi-stiva-chiglia 1000 m. profondità centro dello stretto fogna vulcanica aperta 5 anni fa                          possibili stiramenti dell'intestino terrestre

Villa San Giovanni = febbrilità di 300 lampade elettriche scosse da 18 spessori diversi di vento corrente

danza di pesci divertiti davanti alla ribalta acetilene di una barca peschereccia

Reggio = agitazione di 800 lampade elettriche *(BRANDITO FURIOSO RABBIOSO)* scosse da 20 spessori diversi di vento corrente                odio universale per la luna                scivolare treno fuori dalla rete-ferryboat

# MESSINA

Messina improvvisazione prova generale di

my   feet-bulkhead-keel   1,000   m.   depth
center   of   the   straits   volcanic   sewer
opened 5 years ago                          possible
stretchings of the terrestrial intestine
        Villa   San   Giovanni   =   febrility
of   300   electric   lights   shaken   by   18
different densities of wind current
dance   of   fishes   amused   before   the
acetylene   limelight   of   a   fishing   boat
        Reggio   =   tumult of 800 electric
lights *(BRANDISHED FURIOUS RABID)* shaken
by   20   different   densities   of   wind
current                          universal hatred for the
moon                          train sliding away
from the ferryboat-net

# MESSINA

Messina   improvisation   general   rehearsal   of

una città che sta per andare in scena
indifferenza dell'autore zuccheri e gioie del-
l'atmosfera          altalena di serenate
(3 baritoni 2 tenori) accanimento freddoloso
dell'edera sulle baracche flessibilità del ce-
mento armato in equilibrio sulle furberie rab-
bie della lava fasto di un appartamento =
alcova ➕ baldacchino ➕ galleria di quadri ➕
cucina insaccato in una baracca (8 mq.)
          impossibilità di opporre facciate
altere al vento dello stretto non più di
10 m. di altezza ambizione troncata dei
proprietari          preoccupazione delle
case = stare carponi come lottatori per
non essere atterrate prossima rissa
          presenza del terremoto lottatore
stanco dormente sulla soglia
fumo del vulcano appello lanciato ai ve-

a city that is about to walk out on stage
indifference of the author sugars and joys of
the atmosphere          exchange of serenades
(3 baritones 2 tenors) chilly tenacity of the
ivy upon the huts flexibility of the rein-
forced concrete in harmony with the rabid
cunning of the lava elegance of an apart-
ment = alcove + canopy + art gallery
+ kitchen stuffed in a hut (8 mq.)
            impossibility of opposing haughty
facades to the wind of the straits any
higher than 10 m. truncated ambition of
the proprietors          preoccupation of the
houses = getting on all fours like wrestlers
to avoid getting knocked down next quarrel
            appearance of the earthquake
wrestler tired sleeping on the doorstep
smoke of the volcano appeal hurled to the ve-

suvi stromboli            perfidia delle ve-
getazioni ═ travestimenti del terremoto mi-
naccia di un giardino troppo profumato
odore pepato del pericolo            polve-
riera ✚ volontà ✚ lavoro ✚ comfort ✚
spensieratezza della fecondazione notturna ═
Messina            velocità d'automobili
verso Catania

**70 Km.**

**all'ora**

**trrrrrrrrrrrrrrr**

**chauffeur semisdraiato**
sotto volante enorme che
gira come un mondo patti-
nare pattinare sulle velocità
lavate dagli svolti svolti prati
giardini spiagge scenario di
monti calabresi cono dell'Etna
indaco insenature promontorii

torrefazione scoppiante ✚ velocità ✚ ferocia
delle gomme polvere carbone della strada
sete sete del caucciù cactus

suvius's stromboli's        treachery of the
vegetation **=** disguises for the earthquake menace of a heavily perfumed garden peppered
with danger        powder-magazine **+**
will **+** work **+** comfort **+** thoughtlessness of the nocturnal fecundation **=**
Messina        speed of cars
heading for Catania

**70 Km.**
**per hr.**
**trrrrrrrrrrr**

**driver half-thrown back**
beneath the enormous wheel
that spins like a planet skating skating on the speed
washed by the turns turns
meadows gardens beaches
scenery of Calabrian
mountains cone of Etna
indigo inlets promontories

exploding roasting **+** speed **+** ferocity of the
tires coal dust of the street thirst thirst of
the rubber cactus

futurismo
spinosità
sobrietà   eroismo
spessore   resistenza
solidità
metallismo
antivegetale
300.000   solitudini
solleoni   sabbie   agguati
ghibli bocche occhi bruciore
conquiste africane
Sahara   concentrati

dei
cactus
ascari
offrire
frutti
succosi di
roseo
come
lampadine
elettriche

fe
ro
ce
mente
na
ti
fra
fra   su
nei
contro

*(NERO*
*DURO*
*CONTORTO)*

budelli
torcersi
torrenti
sobbalzi
correre
spasimi
stridere
fumare
di
**LAVA PIETRIFICATA**
sotto
vaste
bambagie
gelate
dell'atmosfera

Futurism
spinosity
sobriety heroism
depth resistance
solidity
antivegetable
metalism
300,000 solitudes
dog-days sands snares
hot Libyan wind mouths eyes sting
African conquests
Sahara concentrates

of the
cactus
native troops
offering
fruits
juicy with
pink
like
electric
lightbulbs

fe
ro
cious
ly

between on
in
against

born
between

*(BLACK*
*HARD*
*CONTORTED)*

bowels
writhing
torrents
jolts
spasms
running
screeching
smoking
of
**PETRIFIED
LAVA**
beneath
vast
frozen
cotton
of the atmosphere

**80 Km.**

**all'ora**

**TRrrrrrrrrrrrr**

> sedentarietà velocissima dello chauffeur semisdraiato nel volante Saturno nell'anello girare girare fare del piede al lontaniissssssimo piedino azzurro delle più folli velocità **glou glou glou** d'aria in bottiglie-orecchie vento ventriloquo

**95 Km.**

**all'ora**

**TRRRRRR**

> abbandono musicale dello chauffeur semisdraiato sotto volante tenere il pedale all'organo russante dei chilometri respirati in un soffio risoffiati lontano

**100 Km.**

**all'ora**

**TRRRRRR**

> respingere con piede destro acceleratore lontananze ╋1000 profondità ╋300000 resistenze della terra alle stroffffinanti velocità offrirsi offrirsi **pan-pan-traaak tatatraak**

**80 Km.
per hr.
TRrrrrrrrrr**

{ speediest sedentariety of the driver half-thrown back from the wheel Saturn with its ring spinning spinning pressing his foot upon the very far little blue pedal of the most free speeds **gloo gloo gloo** of air in bottles-ears ventriloquist wind

**95 Km.
per hr.
TRRRRRR**

{ musical abandon of the driver half-thrown back under the wheel pushing the pedal of the snoring organ of exhaled kilometers in a puff blow again further

**100 Km.
per hr.
TRRRRRR**

{ pushing down with his right foot accelerator distances + 1,000 depths + 300,000 resistances of the earth to the rubbbbing speeds giving giving a **pan-pan-traaak tatatraak**

**tung tung sang panache**

# Stop

(frenamento istintivo sussulto **agonia dello**
chauffeur)                    $\frac{1}{3}$ d'automobile **8**
ruote  brucare  tranquillamente  biondezze  fo-
raggi  ironie  d'un  villaggio  **306**  anni
            stupidità  del  paesaggio  montagnoso
prendere  mio  automobile  per  rovine  vallate
di  Girgenti  stringerlo  nelle  braccia  dei  suoi
ruscelli  alberi  erbe
correggere  bozze  no  no  ecco

# ECCO

le  bozze  come  sono  per  **RIPULIRE**  il
mio  **CARO**  carburatore  superstite

**tung tung zang panache**

# Stop

(instinctive braking tremor agony of
the driver) ⅛ of the car 3 wheels
nibbling tranquilly fodder blondness ironies
of a village 306 years old
    silliness of a mountain landscape
taking my car through ruins valleys of the
Girgenti embracing it in the arms of its
streams trees grasses
correcting galley proofs no no look

# LOOK

the proofs just as they are for POLISHING
my DEAR surviving carburator

from *Zang Tumb Tumb*, 1914

## BOMBARDMENT

every 5 seconds siege cannon disemboweling space with a
tune TAM-TUUUUMB mutiny of 500 echoes in order to gore it
scatter it mince it to the infinite

in the center of these TAM-TUUUUUMB
flatspots (diameter 50 square kilometers) jumping cracks
slashes fists artillery-fire swift Violence ferocity
regularity this low heavy scanning the strange madmen sharp
quite shaken with the battle Fury breathlessness

ears                          eyes

nostrils                          open attentive

power what joy seeing hearing smelling all of the all of
the TARATATATATA of the machine-guns shrieking out of breath
beneath bites slaps TRAAKTRAAK whippings PEEC-PAC-POOM-TOOMB
grotesqueries leaps 200m. height of the artillery Down down
below to the orchestra swamps

sloshing                          oxen   buffalo

goads carts PLOOF PLAFF
horses rearing fleec flac zing zing shiaaack hilarious
whinnies iiiiiii... shufflings tinklings 3 Bulgarian
battalions on the march croooc-craaac (SLOW TWO BEATS)
Sciumi Maritza or Karvavena croooc craaac shout of the
officers dashing to and fro like brass cymbals pan from
here paack from over there ching buuum ching chak (QUICKLY)
chiachiachiachiachiaak up down there around above watch
your head chiaack good                          Flames

flames

flames                                   flames

flames                                   flames

flames                          footlights of the

                                  positions be-

                    flames

               flames
hind that smoke Sciukri Pascia telephones 27 positions in
Turkish in German hallo Ibrahim Rudolf hallo hallo actors
roles        · echoes        prompters ·
                              scenarios of smoke
forests applause smell of hay mud shit I no longer can feel
my feet frozen saltpeter smell rotsmell
                              Kettle-drums
flutes clarinets everywhere low high birds chirping beatitude shadows cheep-cheep-cheep breeze green flocks don-dan-
don-deen-beee tam-tomb-tomb-tomb-tomb-tomb-tomb Orchestra
madmen cudgeling professors of the orchestra the thoroughly
cudgelled plaaaaaying plaaaaaaying Greeeeeat crashes un-
fading specifying reshrrrredding the tiniest noises very
smallest fragments of echoes in the theater 300 square kilometers River Maritza Tungia strewn Rodopi Mountains erect
heights scaffoldings loggias 2,000 shrapnel bits being
stirred exploding handkerchiefs very white full of gold
Toom-tomb 2,000 grenades outstretched tearing up with bursts
heads of hair darkness zang-tomb-zang-tuuum
tuuumb orchestra of the noises of war swelling with anger
under a note of silence
                    suspended in the open sky
gilded spherical balloon surveying shots Kadi-Keuy airport

                         from Zang tumb tumb, 1914

# DUNE

Karazuc - zuczuc

Karazuc - zuczuc

nadI - nadI **AAA**AAAaaaaaaaa (*bis*) *dune duuuuu-*
*uuuune dune sole bruciaticcio dune dunedunedune*

**dum dumdumdumdumdum**

| | | |
|---|---|---|
| precipitato | | derbuka noia bianca ✚ lana |
| abbagliante | **dum** | del rumore del pensiero im- |
| eterno | | |
| abbagliante | **dum** | bottitura sonora del cielo |
| meccanico | | rumore rotativo del sole ri- |
| abbagliante | **dum** | cordi incotonati        tam- |
| consanguineno | | buri delle midolle        tun- |
| abbagliante | **dum** | nel di suoni neri nelle mon- |
| tono maggiore | | tagne  incandescenti  della |
| abbagliante | **dum** | luce |

DUNES

Karazooc - zooczooc
Karazooc - zooczooc

nadI - nadI  ΛΛΛΛΛΛaaaaaaaa  (bis)  dunes duuuuu-
uuuunes  dunes  sunburning  dunes  dunesdunesdunes

                    duum  duumduumduumduumduum

flung           duum      boring white derboukah + wool
blinding                  of the noise of thought sonor-
eternal         duum      out stuffing of the sky rotat-
blinding        duum      ing noise of the sun fluffy
mechanical      duum      memories              drums
blinding                  in the marrow            tun-
inbred          duum      nel of black sounds in the in-
blinding        duum      candescent mountains of light
major key
blinding

Ocra ✚ ottone ✚ cannella 18 kmq

vvvvvrrrriiiiiiiiiiiiiiiiiiiiiiii

| | | |
|---|---|---|
| lacerante universale fibroso tono minore | vluiii vuuliii vuluit vuvuluit | violini gatti scricchiolio di tutte le porte romantiche palle timpani turbini di neve nei fili telegrafici corde del vento tese sul naso dello chauffeur sotto l'archetto tortuosiiisssssimo della strada irruente |
| delicatissimo rampicante stirato | | |

# GIALLOOOGIALLOOO

acredine orina sudore gaggìa sudiciume gelsomino pancia di banchiere arare coi piedi sudiciume sabbiacuscini coricarsisetesete
rumore ✚ peso del sole ✚ odore arancione del cielo ✚ 20 000 angoli ottusi ✚ 18 semicerchi d'ombra ✚ mineralizzazione di piedi negri nella sabbia di cristallo

Ochre + brass + cinnamon 18 km$^2$

vvvvvrrrriiiiiiiiiiiiiiiiiiiiii

lacerating    | vluiiii   ⌐violins cats screeching
universal    | vuuliii   of all the romantic doors
stringy    | vuluit   balls kettle-drums turbines
minor key    | vuvuluit   of snow in the telegraph
   wires          cords
   of the wind stretched upon
very deli-    the driver's nose upon the
cate    very tortuUuUuUuous bow of
climbing    the violent road
drawn out

Y E L L O O O W Y E L L O O O W

bitterness urine sweat acacia filthiness jasmine
banker's belly foot-tillers filthiness sand-
cushions going-to-bed-deep-thirst
noise + weight of the sun + orange scent of the
sky + 20,000 obtuse angles + 18 semicircles
of shadows + mineralizations of negro feet in
the crystal sand

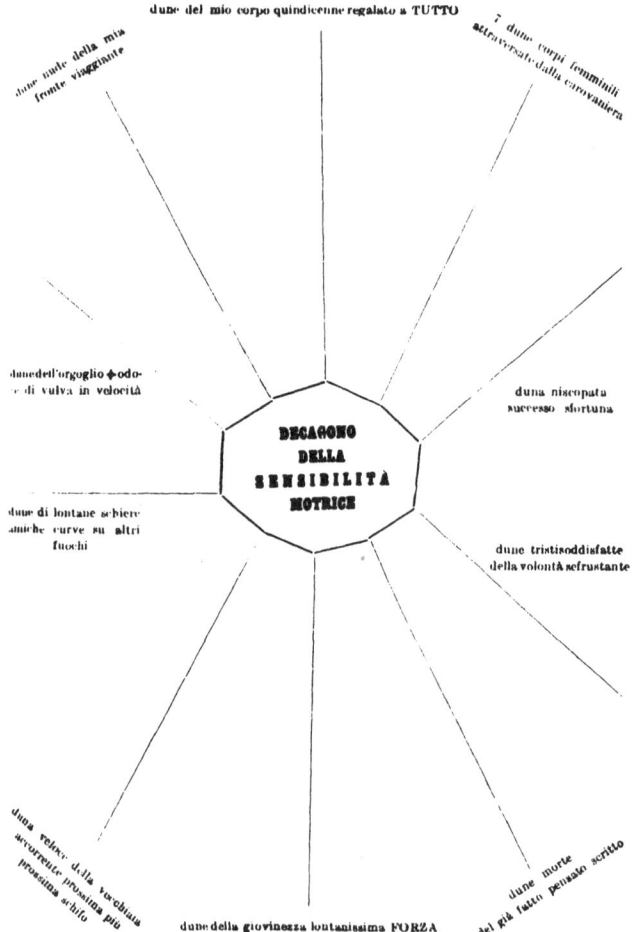

dune del mio corpo quindicenne regalato a TUTTO

7 dune corpi femminili attraversato dalla carovaniera

dune nude della mia fronte viaggiante

dunedell'orgoglio ♦odo- e di vulva in velocità

duna niscopata successo sfortuna

DECAGONO DELLA SENSIBILITÀ MOTRICE

dune di lontane schiere amiche curve su altri fuochi

dune tristisoddisfatte della volontà sefrustante

duna veloce della vecchiaia accorrente prossima più prossima schifo

dune morte del già fatto pensato scritto

dune della giovinezza lontanissima FORZA

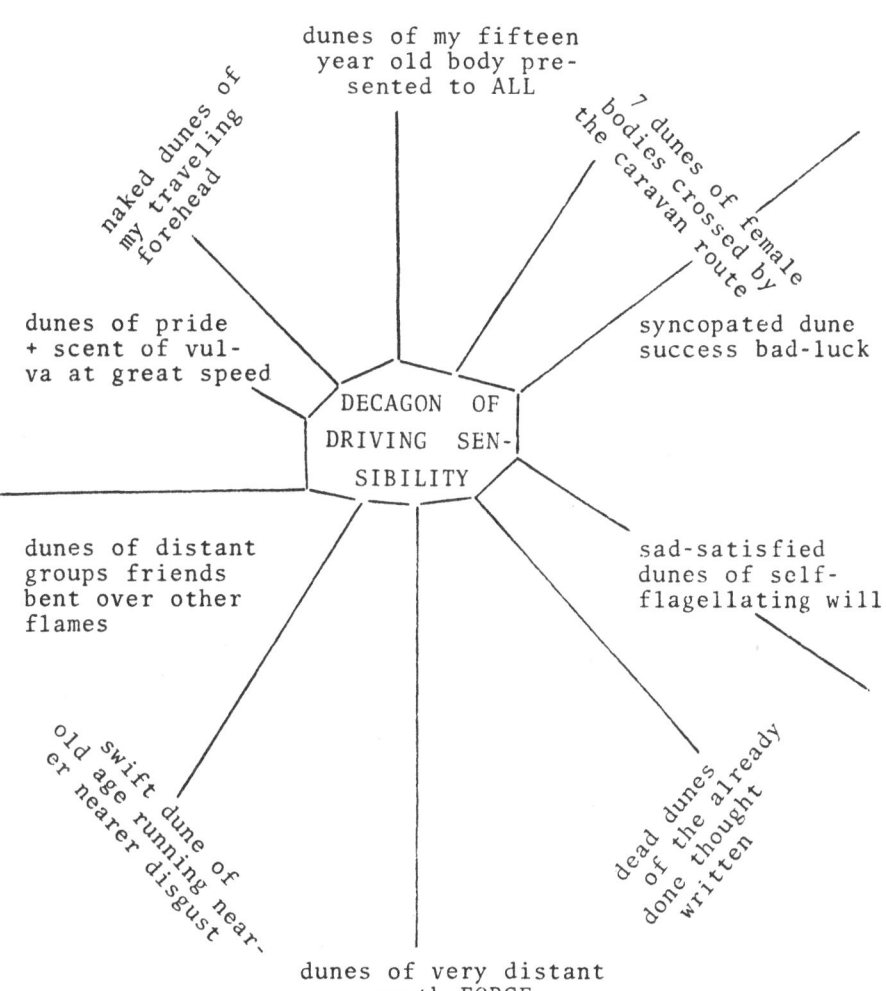

cadenzato
navigante
morbido
maneggevole
minuzioso
intestinale

distanze

distanze
dune
stirarsi
ondulazioni
angoli
angoli

**RAN**

**RAN**

**RAN**

modellare sabbia smussarsi levigare
levigare sonnolenza del vento
paracalli arterie scarlatte gioia di
pagare a un ladro il prezzo del pru-
rito          contabilità delle un-
ghie       ½ Kg di formaggi
     26 Kg. di CARNE FEMMI-
NILE spirali d'un fumo azzurro
   odore di vitello arrosto BET-
TOLA DI ROTHSCHILD (am-
piezza 1000 Kmq) 3 corazzate di
cartavelina    2 capitani di piombo
fuso vomitati dal sole friggente
equatore

sconfinato
abbagliante
ranran
o
quadrato

seeeete

distances

cadenced
traveling
delicate                                          distances
manageable              dunes
painstaking              stretching
intestinal                undulations
                            angles
                            angles
        R A N    shaping sand polishing it off polish-
                 ing polishing somnolence of the wind
                         leather cushions scarlet arteries
        R A N    joy of paying the price of itching to
                 a thief                book-keeping
                 with fingernails        1/2 kilo of
                 cheese        57 lbs. of FEMALE FLESH
        R A N    spirals of blue smoke + the odor of
                 roast veal ROTHSCHILD TAVERN (1,000
                 square kilometers)  3 battleships of
                 tissue  +  2 captains of cast lead
                 vomited by the sun frying equator
boundless
blinding
ranran                            thirrrrst
or
square

rrrrr
sssssssss
rrrrrrr
crucra
crucra
crucra
} urli bianchi concentrici di 14 luuuune impazzite affogarsi lune tonde qua-drate torcersi sbriciolarsi nel pozzo (30 m) di Bu-Fellah (NOOOOTTE) crucracruminare di cammelliiiiiiiiii

**VENTO TORNITORE** { di dune + nervi + rimorsi + nausee + sterchi + barracani in fuga eccentrica

**MOVIMENTO DI 2 STANTUFFI**

**VENTO** { negatore pigrizia iner-zia congelare tutto con stelle letterarie sradica-te dalla carne (NOTTE LIBRARIA) seppel-lire tutto con odore di ascelle materassi di pro-fumi mammelle cotte piacere + 7000 ragiona-menti scettici

**SANGUE** { affermatore ottimismo forza respingere il vento pessimismo caldo o fred-do andare senza scopo per FARE VI-VERE CORRERE ESSERE

Kzrzzic zuozuc
Kzrzzic zuozuc
Rzi nel AAAnnnnnn

```
rrrrr       ⎧ concentric white howls of 14 crazed
sssssss     ⎪ moooons getting drowned moons round
rrrrrr      ⎨ square writhing crumbling away in the
croocra     ⎬ well (30m) of Bu-Fellah (NIIIIGhT)
croocra     ⎪ the croocracruminating of caaameeels
croocra     ⎩
```

```
W I N D     ⎧ of dunes  +  nerves  +  remorse  +
W I N D E R ⎨ nausea  +  excrement  +  barracans
            ⎩ in eccentric flight
```

```
                ⎧ NEGATOR laziness inertia
                ⎪ freezing  everything with
                ⎪ literary stars uprooted
                ⎪ from the flesh (BOOKISH
        WIND    ⎨ NIGHT) burying all with
                ⎪ the smell of armpits
                ⎪ mattresses of perfume
                ⎪ breasts cooked with
                ⎪ pleasure  +  7,000
                ⎩ skeptical arguments
MOVE-
MENT
OF 2
PISTONS         ⎧ AFFIRMER optimism strength
                ⎪ to push back the pessimist
        BLOOD   ⎨ wind hot or cold        to
                ⎪ go without purpose in order
                ⎩ to DO LIVE RUN BE
```

Karazooc zooczooc zooczooc
Karazooc zooczooc AAAaaaaaaaaaaa
NadI nadI

# SOLE OLIATORE UNIVERSALE

MENU D'UN PRANZO DI 6 CO-
PERTI AL LUME DI UNA LUC-
CIOLA

tlac

tlac

cic-cioc

1. Antipasto di kakawicknostalgin
2. Angoscette al sugo
3. rimorschif in bianco
4. presentimentlung allo spiedo
5. grappoli emorroidali
6. orina d'asceta frappée

aih

aiiiii

aiiiii

fuuuuut

sedersi comodamente in quattro sulla
punta d'uno spillo              snellezza
signorile grigioperla del vento che
porta a spasso l'incendio-levrette-ve-
stita-di-rosso

U N I V E R S A L   O I L E R   S U N

MENU FOR A 6 COURSE DINNER
IN THE LIGHT OF A FIREFLY

tlac
tlac
cheec-
choc

1. Antipasto of kakawick-nostalgine
2. Little anguishes in gravy
3. remorse-skiff in white sauce
4. presentimentlung roast
5. hemorrhoidal clusters
6. urine of ascetic frappee

aih
aiiiiii
aiiiiii
fuuuuut

to sit comfortably on all fours upon
the point of a pin          aristocratic
pearl-gray slimness of the wind that
promenades the incendiary levrette
dressed in red

t e rr i BLY   F E R O C I O U S   S U N

S E N T I M E N t a l

blinded
by
tears

above the young explorers deceived
by their loving wives
          solemnity of a cuckold upon
the line of the equator

blinding
with
red
tears

# SENTIMENTALE

**acciecato di lagrime**

sui giovani esploratori traditi da mogli amanti
solennità d'un cornuto
sulla linea dell'equatore

**acciecante di lagrime rosse**

(andante grazioso con pizzicato)

letterina tiepida sudante sul petto dila-
taaaaARSI d'una parola scritta gomito
nudo affusolarsi di nuvola — mano — te-
nue nel caldo 3 giorni
di marcia dune dune dune
COSTA il POSTALE
8 GIORNI GENOVA Parma eccomi
baci zingzing zingzing tradizionale di
un letto di provincia
Karazuc - zuczuc Karazuc - zuczuc sci-
statuneroe zingzingcuic Naldi Naldi
AAAAAAaaaaa zingzingcuic floscezza di cam-
pane bagnate mature cadenti cadecenti

(andante grazioso
con pizzicato)

CAKE-WALK TEMPO

tepid little letter sweating upon the chest
expaansiooon of a written word naked elbow
stream-lining of a cloud - hand - slender in
the heat                                      3 days
of marching   dunes   dunes   dunes
COAST                    POSTAL
 8 DAYS              GENOA  Parma  here are my
kisses  zingzing  traditional  zingzing of
a bed in the provinces
KARAZOOC - ZOOCZOOC  KARAZOOC - ZOOCZNC you
are a hero ZINGZINGCOOEEC NaldI   NaldI
AAAAAAaaaaa  ZINGZINGCOOEEC flabbiness of
bells wet heavy falling fallllingg from
the highest oldddessst branch
odor-of-the-wash-house-acacias-must-worm-
eatenwood-cooked cabbage-zing zang of
casseroles ammoniacal darkness of a tent
full of bedouins
                dunes   dunes   dunes

                                  1914

Tempo di Cake-Walk | daal ramo altissimo antichiiiiissimo
odore-di-bucato - acacie - muffa - legnotarlato -
cavolicotti-**zing-zang**-di-casseruole
buio ammoniacale d'una tenda di beduini
dune dune dune

## LUST

My fifth soul has a beautiful warm orange color. Sumptuous, ecstatic yellow radiation of the African sun upon wind-shaped cinnamon dunes mutatis mutandis, filthy like the drawers of an arab, always in his underwear shirt-sleeves and slippers as he runs over the swift dunes shooting.

Hunger thirst lips sharp teeth nostrils open above below inside all flesh.

Torrid acidsoursickening perfumery of the Souk turk from Tripoli.

Impetuous hard certain optimism that will never give in wishes breaks through opens up plows creates fertilizes.

from _8 anime in una bomba_, 1919

### NOCTURNAL DIALOGUE IN THE
### OBSERVATION-POST OF THE 8TH
### BOMBARD BATTERY AT ZAGORA

It is raining. Two shadows be-
neath the silvery, leaping triangles
of the searchlights. The trench is
terribly white. Petrified convulsion.
The crazed barbed wire seems to shake
its silver grid of rain.
　　　Tell me, do you love Julia?
　　　Why yes, with all my soul. You
too?
　　　Me too.
　　　So very much?
　　　Yup, with all my soul.
　　　Why do you love her so much?
　　　Because, she adores me.
　　　She told you that?
　　　Yup, she's sworn it and proven
it.
　　　She swears it, proves it, to me,
to you, to anyone.
　　　Goodnight, I'm lying down for an
hour, then at daybreak I have to check
the mountain passes.
　　　I'll come with you.
　　　Come? Why?
　　　The machine-guns can do her choosing.
We'll walk together real close, one behind
the other, then we'll be hit together and
Julia will be left with empty hands.
　　　I don't think so. Julia's hands will
never be empty. Goodnight.

from <u>8 anime in una bomba</u>, 1919

PURITY

--Let them go!  Leave them alone!  leave
them!  Come on! Come!
--Where?  Why?  Who's calling me?
I am three meters from the stars. Surely
she calls me.  I hear the liquid diamond frying, burning its eleven rays.
In the twilight I walk upon the clouds'
rosy pavement which covers the valleys.  I can
hear them rumbling beneath my feet like the arteries of a monstrous capital.
I hear interminable trains of cannon-fire
rumbling.  A shiny, hissing hunk of rail is
flung high into the sky, piercing my heart like a
warbler.
Let them go!  Get undressed!  Empty yourself! and rise up!
I'm sleepy.  How can I sleep?  I'm so
susceptible to that fearful voice· I push my
head and shoulders out from the barracks bag
that I carry on my back, like a turtle-shell.
I come out, climb up on top of my shell; but I
can feel my skull atop my brain, another shell-
shack.
Shell, shack or bomb?  Explode!  Explode!
Ice sliding out of my soul, for how many
measureless skaters of the infinite?
That star has its heart set on me, insist-
ing on its sweet invitation with the bestial
crash of its enormous crashing crystals.
--Away away!  Kick away!  kick away all your
thoughts-nerves binding your feet like loving
puppies. Throw yourself upon that mountain-tram-
poline there and ploof, a great dive onto the
plains of the Veneto.
--No!  No!  No!  No!  No!  I refuse to obey
the great Stellar Department of Works!  And this
is no strike!  Tonight I'm working harder than
ever.  All my life's furnaces are firing.  Roar
thump  hiss  of turbines  dynamo  combustion-
engines and electric hearts.  My nerves are
swarming corridors where my senses hammer out
arms-munitions against the central empires of
the sky.
I leave my sense of I to look down from
this mountain height, down upon Rome, like to

the bottom of a well. A well, a swamp to re-
cultivate with new plows, or the eye of a use-
less needle since we no longer have anything to
sew.

That concertina in my bag complains with
shuddering patches violet with grief-anguish like
my cradle. Rocking cradle for the gymnast baby
I'm becoming. I have the tattoo of a beautiful
little face upon my pale chest, so intelligent
and sensual, brightened with a fair complexion.
The tattoo is my wound. The wound is growing.
My body is only its inflamed hem.

Wound or trench? Who defends it? Its tender memory or its cruel forgetfulness? I am
pure and foul like a trench, pinned down and flying, torn and joyous, desperate and serene.

Timid pressure, so hasty and pursuing, of
all the hubbub, black thick buzzings of the night
inside and outside my heart. Perhaps born of
me? I'm an office working day and night.

Put to bed inside my sleeping bag at the
North Pole... I count and recount the four or
five little columns of hatred-silver coins and
the twenty or thirty of love-gold I've saved in
my most secret strong-box.

Yet, outside the immense Bounty of the spend-
thrift Void overflows flooding everything.

I go out and walk with suppleness in the tender silky renunciation of the night.

Gott gatt blav blavv of the coffee in the
flask on my right side.

The aristocratic elegance of night, disin-
terested, profligate.

Upon the summits I fear the lugubrious domination of the great M's Mountains Mother
Moral Malevolence Martyrdom.

The divine abstractions drink me.

I dart ironically but feel caught in the
net of trickling mercury constellations.

I prefer to dive into sleep.

Tomorrow I will recapture with scrupulous
passion that vast, hot, scintillating fabric of
of trains cities tracks villages meadows
roads nice legs called the plain of life which
tastes so good in my mouth.

I am a streaming water that hates the mountains' mystical skeletons. I seek the valleys'
carnal bottoms, the rivers' gossip, and the
songs of the racing wheels.

from 8 anime in una bomba, 1919

WOOD

Satiny mahogany wood crushes of violet from Guyana
Ebony and rosewood from Madagascar coral-wood and
occumé from the Congo mahogany of Senegal
Wood from the islands
Teak from Indo-China and Africa
Tonkin fright
Hardwood
Ironwood
Imperishable wood
Oak and teak from Java

Wood for telegraph-poles
Railroad crossings
Blocks for pavements
Heavy teak logs
Ant-ridden shrill gnashing exploitation of the
widespread woodsmen
We shall make navigable all the African rivers
we improve the ports of embarkation
We shall release rare essences
On the Ivory Coast our railroads will cut through
the tropical forest to transport wood
Indeed we will have over a thousand elephants
to carry the heavy logs
We shall have mountains of rubber and gutta-
percha and mechanical sawmills
Srrrrrrrr
Srrrrrrrrrr
Srrrrrrrrrr
⎛siiiiiiiii
⎜ziiiiiiiii
⎝rrrrrrrrrr
⎝vrrrrrrrrr
My brain grinds out its "Dream of Hard Wood"
and its abominable and voluptuous sawmills.

1920

## PARISIANIZED LANDSCAPE

Languor softness finesse of the lukewarm breeze
Pearl-gray scarf
Charming suppleness of sky-blue blouses on the
distant mountains
3 rosy clouds for lining
A blue stream glides beneath a meadow's green
jacket
Here and there sparkling hues bluing emerald
meadow cherry and straw
The sun composes new reliefs
Amusing fantasies
Soft blends
Plastrons of light very nicely enrich the long
blue shirts with high collars that the hills are
adopting this season
I love these embroidered wool-flocks and moss
which dot the pink and cream blouses of the towns
Wide patterns in thick yellow silk are their
lining
In the middle of this bodice-forest an ancient
gold bell forms a very tasteful pendant
The huge scalloped frills of pastoral songs
engrave the jackets of recently finished hamlets
The straw bonnet-roofs this season are so unusual because the straw is almost hidden beneath the
ornaments of fine literary fogs
The blue skull-cap of the sky displays the
successful shining fringe of picot and velvety
matting
The bonnet-roofs are very becoming on the
faces of the cottages
The ribbon lacing of footpaths continues to
please an imitation straw-hat upon a farm
A morning skirt upon a chapel
A raffia shell and a big rosette of green
ribbon fall over the ear of a hill
A touch of elegance. . . there the watered
silk of the lake enjoys a successful comeback
Hooded capes of tagal and dark crepe over the
towns by the shoreline
Foliage caps mixed with fruits. Garlands of
small brightly colored flowers frame the high plains
of blue tulle
On the tartan straw horizon waxen leather
triumphs encrusted with brightly-colored ornaments

Hooded capes of Moroccan crepe and voile from
Ceylon complement the light dresses of the fleeting
clouds
Blue clouds ever more velvety and pleated
with sleeves of large ballooning cuffs
I enter a village woven fresh and clear
It's the hit of the season

1920

## THE VEGETABLE ORCHESTRA

They became quiet and immediately the forest in-
toned a majestic chorus. High above, the stars were
singing and the glib, sinuous strumming of the great
harps of the lianas rose with their song from one side
of the Oasis. Then the song fell back languorously,
almost delicately elastic upon the ebb and flow of the
foliage. But then, in the foliage, the branches awoke
like frenetic violin bows squeezing all the delight
out of the nocturnal air, up and down with febrile
notes.

How sweet is the last note! It is she, it is
she who awakens all the leaves of the great baobab.
All the leaves play, countless drilling clarinets and
winged flutes, while the trunks offer their organ
pipes to the high winds that channel down to escape
through the roots under the water, from round holes
in long bellowing notes, full of torment, menace, ab-
duction and fate.

Mirmofim said:

--Listen! Listen! How wonderful! We must
take a swim. Let's all swim! And we'll try to imitate the rhythm of this supernatural music while
swimming.

The Untameables began to swim, and swimming
among the caresses of the airy music, they softened
their gestures and trained themselves to the gentleness. So, their jagged and bitten souls dreamed for
the first time of a fraternal embrace.

The nightingales turned up in the high foliage
over the lake in musical squalls. They began a con-
test of trills trills trills trills trills. They defiantly commanded all the musicians of the Oasis to
lift their voices, perfecting the chorus and elevating
it into a more intense musical light.

> tio tio tio tio tix    tio tio tio tio tio tio
> tio tio tio tio tio tix
>> quitio quitio quitio quitio quitio toooo
>>> tinu tinu tinu tinu tinu tirrading
> cicicicicicicicicicicicicicicicicicicicici

--They are the frenzied gigolos of Light!
said Mirmofim.

--Gigolos! Gigolos! Gigolos! sang the

Untamables at the tops of their voices, imitating the
tio tio tio tio tio tio tio tio tio tio tio tio tio tio
nightingales that cavaliered their wooing.
tio tio tio tio tio tio tio tio tio tio tio tio tio tio
They trilled as others laugh cry sigh kiss, then all
tio tio tio tio tio tio tio tio tio tio tio tio tio tio
down heads first with a hail of crystal notes, they
seemed to find the very bottom of the abysses of
human exaltation and pain.
    Dialogues, skirmishes and sonorous duels. The
defeated nightingale admits as much with his long solo
passages. But a conspiracy of notes explodes in the
irritated shade. Laughter landslides. Chords rolling. Pause. In the familiar silence, another nightingale peeps out, sings to test the devotion of the
distant echoes. He sings sings sings sings then drops
through a trap door. A crazy merry-go-round of voices...
    Squaa pipi qui    Squaa glia tidi qui
Cautiously, silence resurfaces. Long suspense swells
with prodigy. And it was the nightingales that imposed it, directing the chorale.
    Now, a nightingale solo. Beak open, he hopped
up up up, a fountain of notes-tears-stars, kisses that
    contio contio contio contio contio contio
dripped back down showering in preciousness a second
nightingale.
    zozozozozozo
    zirrading  tio tio
      tio tio tio
gushed prolixly out of his heart, a warm jet of sonorous
blood that dropped down showering a third nightingale.
He hastened down in a whirlpool of pearls and furiously
selected, chose, discarding and heaping up notes, diamond cut, vibrating melodious gems and melancholy rubies,
drops of blood upon the second nightingale. And that
stream of melody flowed from the first and all the sonorous blood from the second aroused the others with
artistic jealousy. Everyone. Trying and trying again.
To sing better. All of them preferred vast nets of
trilling notes, to ensnare the trees' foliage in the
vast musical sweetness. Each net had thousands and
thousands of hooks from which hung little fishes of
silvery notes.
    And so the nightingales fished flowers of light
out from the sea of leaves, and in their nets dripping
with harmony they hauled in hearts carried-away... Re-
membering... like conches.

from Gli indomabili, 1922

## I'M A LITTLE SPIRAL

Enchanted, the Untameables stopped, and the
dazzling and elastic arabesque immediately uncoiled
to deliver hundreds and hundreds of gold spirals
dripping with bells.  They were alive, dreamily
singing in a fabled penumbra:

> I'm a little spiral.
> My name is Strambinello.
> And you?  And you?  And you?
>
> My name is Pramonico.
> And you?  And you?  And you?
>
> My name is Quagliuzzo.
> And you?  And you?...
>
> Happy hap Happy
> Happy hap Happy
> Hap hap hap Happy
>
> I love I smoke I shiver.
> We are were shall be
> the supreme perfume
> thinking
> at the crest
> of the forest
>
> Motrè mofù moà
> Mòpresu mofuprò
> Sapenchè
> Stàcrein
> Starefò làllà

from Gli indomabili, 1922

I sulk at you
o my life
by whom my life
was ravished
thinking about Buddha
who sulked
at life
All life
meaning
you

1924
from Poesie a Beny, 1971

SUCCESSIVELY

Blue absence                              Successively

       Red will

Pink desires

                                    Sadly gray
                                    in other words
On

               nearby

But

    But

However

        the shadows
prepare a formidable
plot

FOR

        too red

further

                                really
                                TOO BLACK

from I nuovi poeti futuristi, 1925

YES, YES, LIKE THIS, THE DAWN ON THE SEA

(Words in Freedom)

3 corrosive shadows against

the DAWN

the winds working away away kneading the sea so muscles
and blood for Daybreak
EAST     yellow light awry

THEN
an icy green

skidding

THEN

NORTH  an insolent red
  hard glassy noise

THEN   a stupefied gray

The rosy clouds are faraway charms
  carmine fanfares      scarlet explosions
    feeble  no  gray      tomtoms of azure
No      Yes
        NO

        YES

          yes

      yes        yes
                YES


        YES
    bombastic yellow

                Marvel of grays
All the pearls say   YES

Persuasive green-blue discourses in the
enticing bays
The smooth cyanotic Slabs of the sea
tremble with enthusiasm
A ray Rebounds from rock to rock
Wonder begins to laugh in the veins
of the sea
Risk of a blue cloud perpendicularly
over my head
All the sharp prismatics of the waves
go mad
Attractions of reds

no

no

no

YES

YES

YES

soft exchange
of shadows and light

Purely

Expansive repose
unsatisfied half-light

A kindled veil
neckline on the horizon shimmering

ROAR OF GOLD

whirlpool of three shadows in that bay eaten by Sun-
mouth bloody teeth long drivels of gold drinking the sea
and biting rocks

        YES          simply

            YES
            resiliently

    easily
    LIKE THIS

again

   Again
 AGAIN

  BETTER LIKE THIS

from I nuovi poeti futuristi, 1925

## WITH BOCCIONI ON THE CASINA RIDGE
### (Words in Freedom)

| | |
|---|---|
| SLOW | iiiiiiiii |
| VIOLET | (do, musical note) |
| MODULATED | |
| HYDRAULIC | frrrrrrrr |
| COLD | (fa, musical note) |
| ROSE | iiiiiiiii |
| | |
| | frrrrrrrr |
| | iiiiiiiii |
| | frrrrrrrr |
| VIOLET | airiest peaks    advanced swelling of |
| SOFT | the DARKNESS from the bottom up to |
| | peak B 3,000 m. = a polyhedron of 2 |
| HEAVY | violet woods zzzzz + 4 rose snows in love |
| ISOCHRONOUS | peak K 3,800 m. = a triangle |
| | of 3 white winds (20 30 45 degrees |
| MASSIVE | below zero) brawling |
| | iiiiiiiii |
| | frrrrrrrr |
| | iiiiiiiii  volatization of |
| | frrrrrrrr      Casina Ridge |
| VIOLET | peak D 4,000 m. = a triangle of 3 ice- |
| BLACK VIOLET | blue currents (35 degrees below zero) |
| | + 1 violet layer + 2 yellow wood layers |
| BLACK | zirzirzirguuuu musical pressure of the |
| ICED | mountains from left to right |
| | against the easy silver melodic dance |
| HEAVY | of lunar light  musical pressure of |
| | the mountains = extensive cello note |
| DULL | held prolonged without end |
| | D O O O O O O O O O |

ALMOST TOTAL SILENCE

I am the head of a guard post watching over the path-
way curve halfway up     beyond the Italian trenches
within 100 m. of the Austrian trenches

ON THE SUMMIT

OF CASINA

RIDGE

   behind us

{
excellent hoes pick-axes shovels
lifted off the Austrians   pleasure
of using them despite our fatigue
      creec zing zing zang zack
febrile labor       if the Austrians
counterattack us we'll make them
roll back down the mountain
}

TOWARDS

MALGA ZURES

below us

{
quickly by God get going before the
Alpine devils arrive
     creec zing zang
febrile labor anguish of trench-
digging terror of the last escape
in my bones
}

darkness weight ice of the night pensive immobility
of the mountain's prehistoric calm enormous ridges
(volumes and masses immersed in downpour immutability
of the blackest triangle of that mountain a light
palpitating luminous telegraphy) Pa pi Pa pi Pa pi
Pa pi (symptomatic municipal mechanical organized
predisposed bureaucratic)

TOTAL DARKNESS + TOTAL SILENCE

that disintegrates and sends forth breathless noises
frll frrr frrr frrrr they're not dormice Steps of an
Austrian patrol.  Scaling underneath us watch out
let's not pull any disasters with a cough this is
the echo of a cough against that wall

ALMOST TOTAL SILENCE

beneath the enormous overturned cubes of the mountain
panting with crushing noises fu fu fu fu fu (the Arco
train) 8 second rumpling of crrrrrrrrrr crrrr crrrr
carts in flight down the valley dragged by the blue
rumps of horses-terror CHIAAK CHIAAK CHIAAK whips
carrrrrr   crrrrrrrrrrrrtiunttincrr

xxxxxxxxxxxxxxxxxxxxxxxxxxxXXXXXX

crakreek crakrook crakreek crakrook Alpine marshal
scouting.  --Anything new?  No marshal--but if
the Austrians attack, it will be from here, to
the left.  From the right, impossible.  On your
feet, attention!
    Subterranean mooooing of the mountains
whispering toward the earth's center.

    R A M E E E E - RIR O O O O - KLOP

    I get up crak craak of my slow step.  --You
asleep, Funi? (the sentinel to the right) --No.
--Anything?  --Yeah, here. . . Platoon beneath us. .
able to shoot!  sssssssss fsssssssssssss
zirzircariuriu uis uissss frr frrr voluit
sleep darkness weight frost wind-of-frozen-skin.
NIGHT = immeasurable  water-skin fallen down
among the mountains SLEEP

    Riva by Trento = dead geometry + 407 empty
cubes of abandoned houses + the fidelity of 308
remaining cats + the nostalgic meeowing of 608
expelled cats their very long shadows projected
toward Arco along the walls from oblique Riva

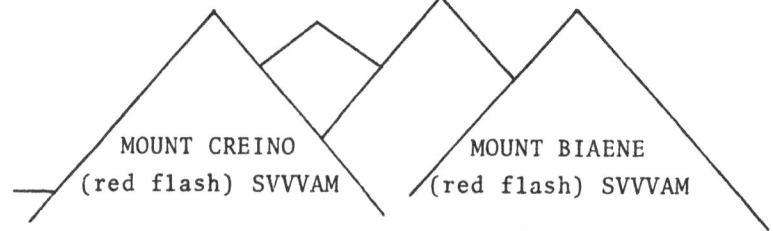

MOUNT CREINO                  MOUNT BIAENE
(red flash) SVVVAM           (red flash) SVVVAM

LEDRO VALLEY ON THE LEFT  MORI VALLEY ON THE RIGHT

peek pak pak pam          peek pak pak pak
tok tok tok tok tok       tok tok tok tok tok
shiaaaaaaaaaaa (echoes    shiaaaaaaaaaaaaaaaaaaa
gravel sea fan skirts     quenching all of its
abandon the very elegant  thirst the African sun
memories of casino-beach) sets lying down
tak tok tok               tok tok tok
panpanpanpanpan           pampampampampam

PAPLUUM PAPLUUM PAPLUUM
(45 Km. range)

ALMOST TOTAL SILENCE

LAKE

GARDA

creek zing crok zang (Austrian
trench below us)
shiaaaaaaaaaaaaaaaaaaa (echoes)     MOUNT
zang zang zing (Italian hoes
above us)                           ALTISSIMO
crrrrrrrrrr (carts down in the
valley)
paplok paplok paplok (horses)
chaak chaak chaak (whips)
fuffuffuffuffuffuffuffu (train
from Arco)

Almost total silence zirzircariuuuu vivicara-timini
tiraaar tonior

PLUUUMBEOOO peek pak pak pak pam tok tok tok
shiaaaaaaa chaaaak paplok chaaak poplok
shiaaaaaaaaaaaaaaa crrrrrrrrrrrrrrr SVVVAM
SVVVAM shiaaaaaaa

(luminous telegraphy in the black Lookout)
PA pi PA PA pi PA pi

from I nuovi poeti futuristi, 1925

## MY ALSATIAN'S LANDSCAPE OF ODORS
### (Olfactory Lyric - Words in Freedom)


Bow! Wow!    A walk    what bliss

FREEDOM            RUNNING

       Ahead behind all around my master Swiftly multi-
plying my master's slow steps with the festoons and garlands of my gallops  Smelling  smelling everything
Inside Holes  protrusions  streamlets  puddles  that
which people call smells a delicious variety from the
immense ocean of odors to smell
      ffff        ffff        ffff        ffff
      1 green smell of tepid soggy grass
      3 gritty smells of damp cold earth
      2 very hot sticky smells    fff    fff    fff
Then away away running among 7 blue waves of
seasmell  Completely bristling with supple peaks
(taking a fine swim in the gaseous foam barking inviting
my master to throw his stick  ploof  swimming quickly
to grab it and carry it triumphantly between my teeth
very tasty mouthful I'm offering to his hands) fff  fff
      Stop!  the full smell of horseshit (very good:
inhaling the whole summer of a sun-cooked hayloft)
      But he's old this horse he's forgotten the immense
fan of green meadows-speed dashing forward to refresh
with hayed and peppered odors the roasted face of the sun
      Let's go on                 A pile of shit with
3 daggers of new smells inside   (Strange! Excellent! but
unless I'm wrong an over-whipped horse whose intestine
oven couldn't shape this pie very well)
ffff        ffff        ffff
      3 violets 1 wild carnation  (what horrors! they're
like the stinks of puppies!)
      Stop!  3 rotten pears 1 bunch of rotten grapes joy
of losing my composure awhile shaking off the weights
measures clasps of cohesion      A puddle of piss (I can
recognize that skittery little wolf Booby) ffff    ffff
      Bree      Bree    Bree   A car? Damn!  I could care
less    I'm sniffing    Now there's my master  calling me
Wolf!  Wolf!     All right!  I'm coming!  I'm coming!
I'm coming!    ffff     ffff     ffff

But wait!  Stop!  STOP!  Finally some PEOPLE  SHIT!
(Delicious!  Divine!)    Bree    Bree  Cars can crush   me!
I'm not moving I'm smelling!
    I'm exhaling with my immense open nostrils
I'm not pulling away  Here I am and here I stay  If my
master isn't looking I'm gonna eat every bit of this
plump musky vanilla-flavored thick rich intimate MAN
smell!
    Finally I will have the venerated soul of HUMANITY
in my mouth  Joy!  What joy  to lap and lap up again and
again  10  20  30  56  times  this mug with my tongue

from I nuovi poeti futuristi, 1925

## MACHINE LYRIC

        Boiler piston    boiler piston    pissss-
tonn      pisssss-ttton    pissss-ttton
        of hot joy PENETRATING the oil frying
laughing  frylaughing its oily oily nostalgia
        Second Piston of WILL - POWER    WILL -
POWER  restrained by too much sensuality-oil (serious
painful badly rhymed) unhinged unhinged continuous
race between two drive belts  (affection  spite)
        3 gears of sad memories lock their teeth
with those of 3 poorly oiled ironies    (stridence
and slowness)
        First exhaust pipe panpantomimepan  pan-
pantomimepan  joy  joy  elegant sublime dancing of
smoke from old sorrows burned  panpantomimepan  in the
pipe shaped like the noisy mouth of a student on
vacation
        Puff!    Puff!  high above a colossal
white globe of ambition-thick smoke!  2 white globes
3 white globes puff out of the locomotive's stack
        Then 3 spirals of weightless gray
fantasies with jauntiness and cheek

            from I nuovi poeti futuristi, 1925

PRECISE POEM


    A man $^{10,000}$ walking with a blond $^{3,000,000}$
loveless purposeless what to do?        climb into
an automobile rhythmed listlessness $^{750}$ the trees
trickling with blue gold and rosy fright are rapid
perfuming brushes $^{1,000}$  $^{8,000}$  $^{800,000}$ bizarre
lust scattered by the wind upright obelisk steering-
wheel beneath the billion hairs that are my nerves
    running flying penetrating the damp tender heart
of silk-meat greedy for space    Clenching the very
manly wheel pitted against the curbstone's virility
far nearby next under      scared SCARED OF CRASHING
$^{1+1=2}$ running into a hole $^{1+1=2}$ breathing $^{1+1=2}$
looking around $^{1+1=2}$ eternity $^{1+1=0}$ full silence +
square expectation + drinking the night He and I She
or another identical thirst doubt satiety
    but our adventure is unique we are on Etna's
slopes two pieces of spent lava triangles spheres
and scalps of black cream figures of chaos


from I nuovi poeti futuristi, 1925

## OLFACTORY PORTRAIT OF A LADY
### (Olfactory lyric - Words in Freedom)

The gate to the city of iron electricity coal
fire smoke speed drinks the endless green of a Spring
morning like a mouth        I am the bitter language of
the city in search of coolness wandering in the sweet
air
      With my eyes closed nostrils open unravelling
with my walking body the very supple and great pulsating
skein of perfumes smells
      It's her        This very soft agile ovoidal vol-
ume of perfumes fresh rosy milky with 3      6        nine
spirals of vanilla fragrances above


      DON'T SEE HER SMELL HER


| To my left | To my right |
|---|---|
| roses | violets |
| roses | violets |
| roses | violets |
| roses | violets |
| roses etc. | violets etc. |
| 20 curves fragrances | 1,000 languages |
| of rose | of violet scents |

Upon the smell
of the wet earth
the fresh warm
sharp and velvety scent
of her breasts
with Italian spirit
advances

Quickening my step
          running
following
          3 spirals
of cigarette odor
          Stop
Warmsweetsour odor

of my gasping breath

in her invisible left hand     in her invisible right hand
swings a bunch of pink        swing 3 banana fragrances
carnations stings and alco-    dissolved by the sweetness
holic romantic flourishes      terror of melting into the
caresses passions etc.         damp shadow of death etc.

          smell of her hair
          compressed by the
          sun brother smell
          of the scorching
          stones

        to my left   and  to my right
        and globally above my head
        changeable arcs of the freshest
        milky fragrance of acacia mother
        infancy weh!  weh!  beginning a-
        gain

              from I nuovi poeti futuristi, 1925

## TACTILE SAILING
### (Tactile Poetry - Words in Freedom)


            Beneath my feet through the vibrating planks of
the steamer a solid sure abstract frozen sea of glass paper
      rolling sidewalk of calm continuous sure resistances
on my face 300 rolls of persuasive and reasonable smooth
silk     chinchilla dawn upon the very long waxy azured di-
van of an ocean with the exciting lukewarm velvet of remem-
brance    reclining    slipping into sleep      on the right
the amorous pressure of pillows (the height of each pillow
50 meters)
            A very hot irritating voluntary wind of granular
silk and chamois skin        brutally broken into pieces
annihilated by an unexpected bombardment of frozen sponges
            Slow humanization of the atmosphere at sunset
    upon the nape of my neck fall 20 forests of female hair
(150,000 heads per forest)
            Here are 300 galloping horses swollen with
lyrical blood rubbing their flanks against my nose
            Endlessly     then with all their speed 2,000
dogs run the straits of my legs
            Pause     immobility
            Apathy
            8 slow kilometers of feathered fans
            From the Southeast an attack of plump elastic
crystals full of soft springing rises up (lasting 10
minutes)
            Tumbling pillows of hot silk (approximately 3,000)
suffocation
            From the sunset's depth 3 houses of blue glass
paper rapidly advance    but over my shoulder 2 towers arrive
unexpectedly (100 meters) of smooth rose silk
which bestride me
            High above the zenith     8 balloons (50
meters in diameter) one white velvet another green wool
from the Pyrenees     all of them caress my cheeks one
after the other
            on the right 2 other houses of red watered silk
(400 meters in height)          open wide like excessive
books and change into measureless perpendicular brushes
as their red watered silk walls bristle with the black
waving arms of their tenant at the window.
            These houses books brushes scrub my forehead

global shock upon my face from all these silk houses-
books-brushes helter-skelter with the wool balloons and
towers
     Pause
     Seal-skin night upon the blue fox sea
     Pause
     3 Parisian tufts upon the commander's lips
standing on the poop in his slicker salted with frozen
reflections

from I nuovi poeti futuristi, 1925

MEMENTO AUDERE SEMPER

III

Thus one day shall you see the Latin water
covered with carnage in your war
and for your crowns have the honor of your
        laurels and your myrtles,
O always reborn, o flower of all the races,
fragrance of all the earth,

Italy, Italy,
consecration to the new dawn
with the plow and with the prow!

                --D'Annunzio

## TWO LITTLE SANDALS AT CAPRI

Upon the hot turquoise of the desert gulf
two red little sandals
Alone...
But every moving reflection is given to you
You in dress of coral
next to my naked brick torso baked
by this heavy red sun
that regretfully is leaving the sea
Words plots shivers suck-marks of the waves
Oscillation
of the two sandals
scale platters of liquid gold
sighing and rising
pensive
Briskly an invisible hand
steals one of the two weights
and I watch it rise into the light sky
To assure the scale's accuracy
I dive like a porpoise
into its wet hair
a soft seaweed or sirens' lace
and I bite
till I draw blood
its rosy neck with the odor
of a freshly opened oyster

Our sandals join
Slow flotsam kisses bathed with tears
Out of spite
and envy
the sun is cut on the thread of the island
Immediately
the delicate shadow curtain
descends from the rafters-to darken
the armchairs of the gulf
Death of a theater!
My box in flames!
Gilded wood and scarlet velvet
drown in the bric-a-brac
of a dead province
Immense, blue face of the sea darkened
a white rowboat like a tear upon its cheek
Our sandals
pointed stretching
towards him

burn like two red nails
in a blond
ray
supreme burnisher of the evening

--Do you want to fly
like a perfect gull
drunk with foam and ready
·for the feast in Paradise?
Put this gentle Milky Way diadem
in your hair
or better these lighthouse gems
with their crossing flames
stolen from the store-window
on the Street of God's Peace

--I prefer my bed
more even than the sea
and much firmer
Perhaps
another time
urchin!
Later, who knows?
The sea would like so much to drink us
some night
slow little sandals
or tears
seeking
the absolute
bottom
nude!

1929
from Poesie a Beny

## THE SACRED MECHANISM OF THE DERVISHES

In a frenzy we shave past the citadel's fat walls,
high, thick, perpendicular coats of desert-colored stone,
rigid recesses with the black mouths of English cannons.

At the base of the Mokatam plateau, a stairway lets
us pass beneath the observation-chamber of the Sheikh of
the Dervishes. A small courtyard of pinasters and dusty
cypresses. With our feet swathed in cloth, we enter a
spacious cavern hollowed out of the limestone. Tombs to
my right and left. In the back, on a square of matting
enclosed by iron grills, three arabs completely wrapped in
black are lying down with their feet pointing to the en-
trance, rolling like printing rollers richly inking themselves.

Outside, on the terrace planted with eucalyptus,
Dervishes in long black kaftans and gray fez wrapped in
white are contemplating, either crouched or seated upon
the marble. Their Master dominates in his green fez and
with the mosquito-netting stretching far off over the
English powder-magazine, over the striped and spiny bulbs
of the dead's cupolas, over the Nile flowing between green
gardens to the orange splendor of the pyramids, each with
its triangle of shade falling like a mantle fixed upon the
occiput.

A factory-like noise calls me back into the sacred
cavern. The Dervishes are spinning like tops with their
arms extended. Their kaftans and white skirts bloom with
the rotary movement. A mystical imploring ingenuity sad-
dens the emaciated face watching their whirling.

Up above, the holy motor vibrates and buzzes. Now
the great stellar steel works perform 15 spins. Filing
the earth. Removing its scabrous surface. High gray
caps without tassels drill the hard air. Occasionally,
like an oil can hovering over them, a plaintive prayer
pacifies the rusty strains of the arabian musical instru-
ments.

The ragged, heaped-up orchestra cries:
--We imitate the rhythms of the universe!
--We mechanize the cogwheel-man of the planetary
system!

One of the human lathes stops. Two. Five. Sweating. Dropping down, one of them curls up near me upon his
mat. The stronger ones lovingly cover their older compan-
ions with their cloaks, then all begin to pray, their

legs crossed. Now I perceive only the Master, the only one
to remain on the mat while the others danced. He listens
to their prayer, his gray fez over his ashen face. He
rises. They rise. They follow him with their long oooo
like a siren in the fog upon the Thames.

from Il fascino dell'Egitto, 1933

## BUFFALO THOUGHTS

The train brushes a banana tree, thick with living emeralds and gushing gold fringes, like a chased burglar. The canals stretch out high above the lateen sails that appear like sharp knives.

Camels and Fellahin harmonize their own curves with those of the villages, all very rich and pregnant with plains.

The train's rhythm is padded with fat clods. The car relaxes my body's tremors and captures it with its vibrations between the flies and the warmhumid breath of a crouching water buffalo who draws her head like a giant turtle out of the immense muddy shell of the plain in order to watch over a tipsy crowd of white Arab graves.

The buffalo chews:

--I am the daughter of the black earth and the gray Nile. Lying down I look like a pile of mud. I sculpt my-self in getting up and right away my rump and horns con-tinue the profile of the low roofs overloaded with straw, rags, kids, oven-domes, earthen smokeless pipes; I love the stillness just a few steps from the rails and the road. I will not lift my snout for the passage of some Fellah who, seated upon the flanks of his undulating camel, stares with-out even noticing me and who doesn't deem worthy of his glance either the goal he wants to reach or the Delta that smells like the sweat under his arms. You will never breathe an atmosphere as rich with germs as this one of mine. This air is evaporated lime. It presses against your cheeks like a tepid sponge. The long, glossy ibises, sweeping the black paths or the brilliant green of the meadows, incense the sky with the good earth!

Meanwhile, the blue sky has become red-hot and small scattered clouds of silver have appeared, more and more illumined and suspended like lamps above some invisible divinity. A premonition of water. Anxiety of the light. Thirsty brilliances of the rocks.

from *Il fascino dell'Egitto*, 1933

## BRAWLING TACTILISMS OF FERTILE EARTH

## AND BARREN VITRESCENCE

An acute sensuality heats my lips and nostrils.
My nerves, extending themselves, have covered the wheels
of my car and transmit the varied tactile blisses of
my tires.
A fat road of black earth and mud. Fleshy,
greasy, saturated with germs. Both sides sink down
into the distance of the low countryside's turbid pools,
skeletal irrigation wheels tortured by skeletal horses,
bronze buffalo inserted in the emerald meadows, ecstatic
ibises and flying tufts of pigeons.
My skin, oiled by the Nile, abruptly trembles
upon the edge of a new tactile world, completely dry,
glassy, metallic: the desert!
I start in upon the sultry padding of the horizon
of sand. Sahara. On the donkey my burnt hands enjoy
the dampness of his sweaty back beneath the saddle. The
air is dry. A drop of sweat shines preciously like a
flawless pearl upon my wife's forehead who looks like
the Queen of Sheba among the blackish, breathless and
bawling snouts of the ass-drivers.
Trotting along like babies upon an infinite mat
of sand. These are its sucking and receding affections.

from Il fascino dell'Egitto, 1933

SWIFT SPAIN AND FUTURIST BULL


1.    Against Forbidding Wind, Commander of the
      Forces of the Past


2.    Problem:  How to Package a Space X in a
      Time X


3.    Spanish Music of Wheels Upon the Headstrong
      Strings of the Guitar Road


4.    The Bull Fight Against Tenacious Symbols

1.

Against Forbidding Wind
Commander of the Forces of the Past

We knew that in those 700 kilometers between Barcelona
and Madrid the Forces of the Past under the command of
old Forbidding Wind were waiting in ambush for us.
Departure at two in the morning in a fast car. Diving
into the jolting white black loom of electric lights
intersected by frightened shadows. Andante maestoso.
Oiled crescendo. Uncertainty of pianissimi desires on
the surface of the street over the holes and cobble-
stones. Amorous cadences repercussions of tires dreaming of the bare legs of children between the rackets
of angels in a sportive paradise. Screams of scorched
metals and wheel moans trembling in harmony upon the
taut spatial-temporal cord that ties me to my talk on
World Futurism tomorrow in Madrid.

Stop. Crossroads. The malignant half-shadows are
gossiping:
        --What are you looking for? Nothing to show
you. Do you claim without stopping to know our orig-
inality, to measure the capricious traces of time upon
our skin? We will throw you the usual banal aspects
of old patched and restored Europe for food!
        With a dash on the dark plain. An hour empty
of form, color and thought. At a turn I enter with
an ironic yellow moon into the cleft of a burnt-out
planet.
        Spectrality of gray ravines armed with flower-
ing metals. Sullen fatalism of a wild poisonous herb.
Vexation of a grotto stuffed with shadows. Dark massif.

Granite regrets machine-gunned by the merry speed.

Old Forbidding Wind throws himself forward howlhowlhowling, rolling big big barrels filled with drunks,
brawls, staggerings and wine cellars disembowelled by
cannonfire.
Some time back he razed to the soil every tree-
restraint or silence, and he enjoys this.
He falls freely into the gorge, dancing wildly,
coughing up prehistoric extra-terrestrial swears and
goes on and on and on recounting muddy conspiracies of
swamps against snowy peaks, chattering sea-greens against
passions of stars, revolutions of tropical locks against
a disdainful aristocracy of polar keys.


Whiteblack
Whiteblack
Triangles.


Old Forbidding Wind postures in his elevated tunic
of bronze black with thundering folds, his belly full
from a slaughter of convents, windmills and Arab citadels.
His long priest's hat, plush and tasseled by clouds,
zooms up to form an open beak that snips the trembling
infinite with his funereal bignose.


Howlhowlhowling

I roared:
--Forbidding Wind, I'm not afraid of you!  I'm not
frightened by your horrid hordes of putrid green nostalgia that you suck up out of the swamps!...  Do you think
you can suck me up too like the moaning soul of a cathedral through its spires?  Ah!  Your stink of soot doesn't
stupefy me!  Your lips must now run over the smoking
chimneys of Barcelona which you take for a rustic syringe
or an altar of wax candles to snuff out.  I challenge
you, broken fire-extinguisher wandering in search of
candles!


Wwwwind


Wwwwind.


As his first reply, Forbidding Wind hurled upon
the car an entire supply of military blankets necessary
for a Spanish expedition into Russia.
Then, with a deep breath he screamed:
--I hate your geometric splendor and your reflecting polish!  Get out!  I will blind your headlights!
I will stuff your gear-box with sand!  I will suck your
carburator!  Ice up your magneto!  I will inflict upon
your wheels my unhinged law of disorder confusion
chipping dribbling snivelling oozing litanies ruination
agony agony aagony
aaaaagonnyyyy!...


Aaaaagonyyyyyy.

Burial.  Rabid convulsing of the radiator eyes teeth
lips under the hard whirling gag.  Suffocating.  Frying
irascible oils.  Precipitous catarrhs exploding in the pipe,
escape of spitting injuries.  Thuds of proud connecting-
rods.  Laughing laughing gears.  A billion ardours in
three points of steel regulating the headstrong ton upon
the tires.  Squeezing the street, prying it up.  Frenetically chewing the dust.  Weight.  Light.  Freedom.
Fiiiinally  getting a move on again.


Aaaaaaaaaaah!


Re-sur-rec-tion.  Running running, then stop.
Pause to clean.  Below the wild Wind belches ranrancors
against the parked car, its hood up, oases of white-
fringed lights drinking the mechanical curve bordered
with gold.  Plugged gasline.  Blowing hammering filing.
Tingling regrets and the slow buckshot hitting our legs
buried beneath the rubbish of our suitcases filled with
their commodity fresh caressable laundry now imprisoned
unreachable.


irrrrrrrrr.

136

Outside the clumsy dust becomes a pillar that boxes
the steel and glass with shaggy brush-hands.
Felicity: a long flash of vermilion infancy. It is
Dawn. Quickly quickly diligently sprinkling sprinkling
the whole sierra and our thirsty carburator with a rosy
gilded blond sherry.


rose


gold          gold


emerald


orange.


Lurch of the engine. Awaaay. Unchaining itself.
Wriggling free from the thin arms of bony bandy solitude
and the hairy armpits of bitter grasses.


rrrrr
bittttter

Hovels leaning to the right and the left burst
their little wooden balconies in order to drop their invisible but sensible phantoms of the Past onto the car.
    They clamber on my face growing veins arteries there
his yours mine.
    I mutter:
    --I'll never see you dirty hovels again!  My eyes
will never again fondle the stitches veins gradations of
your so humanly wrinkled plaster!




                        Whyyyyyyy?



    Angrily, Old Forbidding Wind followed us in the Sun.
    Suddenly the ochre houses, with their roofs lower-
ing out of sight, flatten out sculpted into the ochre of
the gibbous sierra.  Heroism.  Stubbornly resisting holding firm against the vendettas of the Wind all the re-
silient rifles and flying machine-gunned bullets of the
thrown stones.  Hastily painting my face vermilion green
rose to cast a spell upon our enemy.  Growing apprehensive
digging in like Bedouins in the dirt to deceive the worn-
out projectiles and expelled pleasantries.  Forbidding
Wind turns up with a scattering of bronze leg-kicks then
jumps to his feet enormous tapering he disappears into
the Zenith.  Pause.  He returns: monumentally tall above
the smooth vanishing curve of the earth, one of his long
tortuous arms grabs and shakes 2 powerful rearing mules
staggering beneath their saddle-bags filled with olives.

The sun has forever welded together with fire the doors to the Peones and Camineros cubic shelters. Where have these wayfarers gone?

Perhaps already snatched by a dust-turbine, they travel in the sky freed from their weight and having their faces endlessly powdered.

flying in the white

white

white spiral

Between two yellow slopes plowed by the slowest mules, the bouncing car squeezes the enraged road which rises up globulously white in order to bite the car on its ass.

Dragging hoarse groan of a locomotive seduced pressing toward the plaintive conventual dingdong of a belltower in the tiny station stop. Duel between Forbidding Wind and the super-civilized automobile that desires to round round every curve breast thigh knee shoulder of the humanized sierra.

vvvvvv

rrrrrr

vvvvvv

    Running.  Very slow midday.  Rapidly pursuing after-
noon.  Dozing off like two grandfather clocks upon the backs
of fleeing robbers, we reach the bloody-red olive press of
sunset with the loaded mules.

               little by little  up   up   up

               little by little  down  down  down


Frozen savoury plateau of space.
Opening the beak and wings.  Meditating.




                    Expanding

                 Pride of heights

                flying virginity

The last purple muleta of the sun drives Forbidding
Wind crazy, a raging bull kicking up burning dust in the
arena of mountainous ripples full of echoes from aficion-
ados applauding with their prickly-pear hands.
    Rosy clouds descend in skyblue mantillas and plumed
fans upon the stony borders embroidered and striped with
violet.  That beggar seated on the little clay wall pro-
tecting a patch of faded yellow wheat does not look at them.


            cruuc crac cruuc crac
    of a piece of hard bread in my mouth
            the itch in my right
    leg        Ah!
    How that wire of grass trembles!


    The fresh infinite kisses my cheeks.
    Who will save that little snowy flock seized
vortically by the uprooting mantle of the Wind?  Joy!
It's twisting, it's leaping: it's free.
    But he retakes and voluptuously strangles the
full white cloak of their horizon desperation.


            A second joy

    Joy              6 sharp rose joys

      But a black momory abruptly
    stabs 5 of them

Perhaps that humble flock wanted to hear the
Spanish reed-pipe, human cord of a bow without arrows
grazing the bloated bladder of the setting Sun and
the quivering reed of a finished day below it.
   In the restaurant-car of that train:
   --Quiere mas?
   --Un pochito mas, chews an Argentine lady.
   The fat husband then selects from his own plate
of meat saffron rice a delicious mouthful of wild veal
boundless prairies the oceanic waters of Parana, and
adds it to her full plate and to the high enclosure of
her burgeoning breasts that, laughing rice and yellow
sauce, stick out of the windows to militarily occupy
Castile. Everything, except a slope that extends its
starving tongue to the white sky.

2.

Problem: How To Package
A Space X In A Time X

A little bell from the station almost eaten by the darkness
beckons the last friar in Mexico glued to God by evening
prayer and anticlerical rifles to the refectory.

Here we are, we shall stay.
Come on if you dare.

Sudden and forced stop.
Time and Space, which I was holding all wrapped
up in my clutching hands, suddenly tear the lid.

Prompt terror

Logics tremble

Irritating immobility of the automobile before the onrushing problem to be solved: I must add the 400 kilometers between here and Madrid to the box of four hours between now and 9 o'clock set for my lecture on World Futurism.

This box must somehow hold these 5 villages shaped out of the red earth and those precious precious waters feverish silver currents set into the brown plain.

So I shove shove between the walls of the box all of strong gray Spain mangled with its long muscles plateaus militarized with metallic veins and gradations violet gold blood purple iron copper sapphire.

That hump of camel or sierra holding 2 African villages hanging in its valleys stubbornly refuses to squeeze into the back.

Luuurch of the automobile eating the road.

Who can say if it will digest the entire piece swallowed?

Second luuurch: I must cram into this box of 1 minute the three kilometers between here and that indispensible gasoline in the next village!

Anxiety

of the driver's

mouth

Solidarity of flesh + steel

Puuush. Not bad, I was able to close the lid.
Shit! 300 meters are still out of the box. Not only;
20 castle keeps of limestone and 2 sand ramparts riddled
with fuming life also got left out. Dancing in my hands,
here they are, stolen from the Wind. What can I do with
that skeleton-pie of grimy hovels the tearful lights
lament beneath the Cathedral's crushing tyranny?


The engine shares in the

violent arithmetic reckoning



I see our automobile in a dream scurrying like a
mouse over the 2 kilometric steps of the plateau.








Climbing


rrrrrrrr

Problem 3: To try to squeeze the 23 kilometers between here and Alcanitz into this other box of 5 minutes. The scorching inches of the 4 tires squeeze.

Yelping of 2nd speed increasing.

It's uncomfortable gathering strength in this position.

If, by some miracle, these 23 kilometers fit into these 5 minutes we'll be saved! Saved? From what pain? The pain which the crime of lateness deserves!

Serious penalty!

Onward, with strength still we try.

I puuush the 23 kilometers. Get in! Get iiiiin! Then quickly, down with the lid. Oh, no! 6 poor kilometers have been amputated, contorted and numb, with 3 mule-drivers gagged by a bulky scarf of wool wind sierras and clouds.

To take refuge from colds in Paradise!

3.

Spanish Music of Wheels
Upon the Headstrong Strings
Of the Guitar Road

Lofty Arab clouds made of pink fine sugar, in the shape of dromedaries loaded with gold and horses frothing frame the olive pallor mascara of twilight; and below the guitar plays to the road's many curves held tightly by the broad sierra with its convulsed stony arm.

Downwards, the automobile and its wheel, notched strumming fingers on the right hand, pluck at top speed the taut long strings upon the umbilicus-valley of the guitar-road.

Above the thumbs, first stars clawed with a left hand spasmodically press the musical pulse of the road, all feverish in sonorous nerves, all exploded with drunken affection.

Desperate lassitudes.

Aggressive leaps of notes between snatches of deep water sucked with tearing sobs.

Quickly the ring finger suffocates under the thumb weighing the pathetic treacherous pouring out of a crying note which dashes forward boozing it up with a desert regret.

Keep quiet!  Who is groaning so disgracefully? Maybe that dog we flattened a little while ago?

Yes.  Yes!  Poor dog!

Or maybe that beautiful crying dirty gypsy girl of the
night who makes backbone neck and brains spring up
shamelessly from behind?
        She sings:
        --He came, he smiled, he kissed me and left me
the gift of the black flower of death!  But first he
was happy to trample my heart beneath his feet with his
slow ruthless pleasure and ... mine!


                    Aaaaaaaaa

        ooooooooo  Aaaaa

            rrrrrrrrrrr




        Silence, ever the composer, abruptly covers all
of Spain inflicting its firm violet pause.




                Siiiilence

            Void.

Old Forbidding Wind is offended.  The violent
fellow leaps out of the Sierra all nibbled polished
skeletons and falls upon fleshy Madrid of marble meat
fruit glassware wheels silk and jewels of electricity.
Madrid vibrating with rich fast automobiles seems from
above like a roaring estuary of sumptuous ice broken
loose by the Thaw.  Rounded sparkle of varnishes in love
with blue.  Icy dancing reflections.  Soft tender
affectionate quilting in flight and cadences beneath
the smooth waists of women sculpted by rare delights.


To possess all of them!


Senoritas caballeros in the Residenzia de Estudiantes.
Spanish slow-motion looks upon Parisian screens.  In
crooked red mouths Russian tea mixes with Andalusian
pastries which deliciously crumble like Arab villages
beneath the moon's shining teeth.
This sticky sweet from Seville holds out and bestows
its disquieting flavor after a slow squeeze between the
lips:


cheec chac lap cheep
gott glu of sea tongues
against the palate of
Gibraltar's grottoes

--Marinetti, el dio de la velocidàd, non ha freia!
--Se comprende, answers a profile of sculpted ivory
furnished with weapons by two slow black eyes beneath a
very white brow of the Moroccan evening.  Marinetti porta
nell'aumovil el peso del ciaro de luna.  Viaha con sua
mujer, la muy hermosa pintora e escritora futurista Benedetta!

(Applause)

After 20 hours and 600 kilometers with nothing to
put in our mouths we run like an endless song over the
greatly shimmering strings of the guitar-road.
      Strumming, coarse hail of gripping fingers upon the
swept and plucked strings.
      To conquer conquer the sad Infinite Emptiness!
How?  With what weapons?  Our choice: a steady great rosy
absolute Love which fastens itself with watchful facets!...
But if the Infinite Emptiness resists, what then?  Knock
out its bottom with the immense bloody fist of a proud
creator!  To make, to fill the frayed Dark Void with an
Astonishing New Construct.
      And if the Infinite still resists?  Diligent kisses
caresses prayers enfeebling its hardness with the sweet
unguent of rending violet twilight tears renunciation...
No good!  That is a death before dying...

The tired driver collapses with sleep in the dying
headlights, hooked to the exaggerated wheels which become
the pivot of the circling firmament of constellations and
rushing roads from above.  Horror of being forced perhaps
to explain World Futurism to the stones of the dry stream,
face down upon the earth's black mouth.

Yet from above the Arab lament is carried to us
soaring over the taut strings of the guitar-road.  It flies
to the clearest voice and, climbing ever higher with reels
flourishes curls and aerial note contortions, desires to
fashion evermore surprising and foolhardy arabesques atop
the most desperate summit of the Zenith's heart.


high above

higher still


Now it spins.  Desires does not desire.  Laughs
weeps shivers.  Resists.  Then loses support, slips and
falls.  It rises again, then tumbles headlong.  Attempts
to hold on, cannot and falls down splitting silver and
bronze strings in a great tearful blazing arrogant death
of notes.

Dead?  No!  Conquered?  No!  Here rather is the
wounded voice roused rebounding, a sharp sharp blade ach-
ing and savage rummaging through the sand-choked sores of
every living mendicant in the desert.


No!  No!  Mercy!

Mercy!

Mercy!

Old Forbidding Wind amicably lulls the lament with
full rhythmic howls that change to motor roars beneath the
rocky shoulders of the sierra. Then they take off all
stream-lined and metallic, and fly with aluminum wings to
a Gypsy who rules on the third diamond roadstead of
Betelgeuse.


aluminum


steel

diamond


metamorphoses of the engine


I declaim this freeword poem to the natives of
Madrid while Old Bitter Wind, geometric lover of the Escurial, surveys Castile with its kilometric limbs.
Plastic dynamism of an airplane
flying on the cubism of the Escurial


Boccioni

Picasso

The Arab limestone forts shrink under the burnous
of woolly darkness.  Along the embankments of Toledo's
walls the leanest Christs of  El Greco stretch out like
mother of pearl smoke punctured by the joyous winged golf
balls of Basque champions before the Queen's eyes.  The
gold slopes of mysticism are enclosed by their fog coffins.
An anarchic beast's lair explodes with heat beneath a bul-
wark of living flesh, without distracting the flight of a
Yunkers carrying the council president over Guadalquivir.
The new electric lights of Barcelona and Bilbao prevent the
old soot of Catholic funeral pyres to refoul the Spanish
horizon.

4.

The Bull Fight

Against Tenacious Symbols

An Historian writes:
A bull-fight of "novellados" with the foolhardy inexperience of its "banderilleros cappeadores picadores matadores" beginning and anxious for glory has the fascination of endless risk of death and the value of a relative impartiality toward the bull and his assailants.

Waves of crying applause abuse shouting up and down throughout the seat tiers padded with felt hats and white shirt-sleeves beneath a frenzy of polychrome fans which excite black glances and the shouting dazzle.

Heaven of red-hot steel tinted occasionally with blue paint. Fire shower in the skull. Panting beneath the scorching penetration of hat-pins and female nails by an eternity of executioner sunlight. It will never set.

With an abrupt gnashing of its metallic jaws the toril's mouth opens and breathes a fresh rush of boundless meadow land and a black block: the Bull.

Skein of shadows. His abundant horns are adorned with white airy horizons. The odorous flanks of solitude and wild carnations. His rump radiates plump dung like melted gold. He nervously scrapes the sand with his forelegs and throws some against his sides.

Meanwhile the banderilleros unfurl their races of
yellow red green silk in order to tease the black beast into leaps jumps.  Public ironies flog a youth who waves two
banderillas in his raised hands, aiming them at the bull.
A leap, to plant them in the withers, to avoid a
butt with a prompt twist of his buttocks, and away!
--Muy bien, Paquito!
Applause and laughter.

Flights of dark glances from behind the conventual grating of gold fans

The rosy flesh of the sand vibrating to impress the
necessity of killing or dying stretches out beneath the
motionless bull.  The barrera separates the death zone
from life.
The Estribo, sidewalk of ousted piccadores, magnet-
izes the legs of the banderilleros.

Grimaces and waddlings of adolescent Danger.
Invisible.  Only his solar locks reveal him.

The bull dashes forward with pointing horns. To the
right with the fury of his hind legs. Then to the left,
against an orange cape. Vain trajectories. Stop. Sniffing. Concentrating every smell in his horns. Clarifying
them with a little node of crafty instinct, while a cardi-
nal's pomp of capes offered fleeting glide about diabolically.

red

   red

black

BLACK

NEGRO

violet        red


In the seats, in the equatorial pulp of the public
sliced by the razorous sun, there stretches a sticky
tactilism of heavy breaths, nauseous odors, neurasthenic
elbowsand sweaty cushions.
The first piccador advances heavily into the arena.
Leather-like. Monumental, with phoney tresses and sombrero
laced with sun, the cavalier is fit on his skeletal horse
of wood. Mystic fat book with metal boss locks and aphor-
isms of Torquemada. The mournful rain of centuries drapes
this Don Quixote, his lance resting across history.

Eternity.

Rugged voices and clusters of blue heat rain oblong sparkles and burning tears.

With sharp flashing moves vendors in white slippers hurl paper bags full of roasted nuts to spectators who a-muse their teeth.

--Pobre toro!

Who said that? Maybe they flew out of the mouth of some mendicant fallen in exhaustion at the cross-roads of my desert veins that adore poor beasts...

Pobre toro!

Pobre toro!

I alone truly hear the Bull's voice:

"I admire you, oh inexperienced but brave Novellados. Your effort to capture glory impresses me! You bounce like hugh rubber balls. I would like to drink with you while moving fast all the sweet and tart perfumes of my Andalusia.

"To stop together in a July sunset among the terra-cotta myrtles, wild mint and resin, as the full moon sits fully in the arcs of my horns, savoring the rapture of the hay... But why do you want to humiliate me with those banderille? Don't run away behind the burladeros. Do I frighten you that much? You're all a bunch of thoughtless cocky, vicious kids, dreaming of kissing two stars at the same time with your one mouth during your easygoing flights!"

Now, the bull is silent, but during the uproar his belly revealed an implacable wrath against the Absurd which tortured him. His withers are bound up in a purple viva sputtering a gilded crackle among the long rays from the solar grill.

Absurdity

Long dagger-thrusts of fresh sun
into the wounds

He continues:
"And you piccador, a symbol of life's toilsome maturity, you seem like the surviving arch in a convent destroyed during a march against my impetuous, satanic horned animality! Can you blame me? I look like a parody of some mountain when I fertilize the heifers with all the power of my dagger.

Yes! Listen to him!

"I simply lift both the horse and the rider way up
high on my horns and shake them while easily carrying them
like a tree shakes a terrified roost during a blizzard.
And then I throw them down.  The piccador is beneath the
wreckage of his horse.  They lift him back up pretty quickly, but between his legs a red fear drips.  I disembowel
him with my second butt.  Try to stitch him back together,
stuff his open sides with hay and sand.  I'll finish him
off with a third blow.  And now, for you my happy-go-lucky
horses to drag him away to the blowing of trumpets and the
kicks to harness bells and red but bloodless banners."


Black power in a ringing

pink and sparkling ringing


The bull pauses again, his horns standing silent,
resolve become stone.  Then he drools some kind of home-
sickness:
"I wish I could go lie down in the tall grass and
soothe my thirst with some shoots... but I'm surrounded!
Another ambush stretches around me with splendors riches
honors jests and gaudy sumptuousness.  I can smell their
crooked perfumes of power and senile glory.  Again I must
assault the triumphal capes of blinding red and orange.


Why are you going?  Stick around.  We love you, so
much is everything sweet within us...

Life strokes my horns thus, with its pieces of deep
blue ocean, emerald clouds, volcanos of sulphur, avalanches
of violet silk for pretty blonds, a procession of brunette
queens, rhythmitized  by tramping mules...

It's late. It's almost night in the caves of the
heart.  Bahhhhh!   To laugh laugh laugh through the wild
grasses in the sun...To keep laughing forever!

With a jolt I am free of all the banderilles and
flies that had cast anchors in my hide.  Here's another
piccador!  Damn that annoying green cape.  Now this other
silver one is wrapped around my horns!  So what, I'll drag
the cappeador spinning.  He falls, gets up and defiantly
slaps my eyes.  Why, I'll fall on him and trample him.
Ugly meat-bag full of nails."

I'm on fire!  Oh my fresh distant youth...
        Green spasm!

                Softviscous.
(Andante con pizzicati)

The tide of mocking cries is swelling in the seats:
--Non es una corrida!  Es una capea!...  Malo!
Malo!  Ladron va al Mexico!

Malo!

Maaaalo!

Hisses

The shiny red blood streams out around the sword
driven in like a cross into the cavity of the withers.
The wounded but unconquered bull slavers his white lizard-
like tonque and shakes convulsively.  His sex is a black
hairy tassel wagging beneath his agitated belly and sides,
sucked up and shaken by the gust of hatred terror death.
With his threatening horns aimed, he concentrates and a-
gain delivers his tangling revenge in the flapping blaze
of whirling capes.
    A tiny blue sky of flying doves in peace silence
kisses liberty shudders over the contracted, quivering,
muscular haunches.  Collecting gold ingots all over the
panting chest and sweating back of the matador.  Festivity
in deep red frozen into Seville's ice-cream and on the
capes readied then taken by either the wind or by servants
with coral dress coats.

--Es una corrida aparetosa! sighs a senorita whose
rose sequin fan reflects the bull with a row of seats
bristling with fierce afficionados.

                             gold

    gold

                             gold

    gold

        gold

    Finally the chosen man disguised with his muleta
aims his sword at the bull's withers who watches and mur-
murs
    "Why are you hiding your sword which I've wanted
for so long? Ah! Bad luck has stuck it to me!
Obliquely!

              uuuuuu

    uuuuu               uu

Good thing I have so much blood I can squeeze the blade and check it. Can't you hear the hammer of my heart beating so so so much? My wound will absorb it! Ah! Ah! I want to lavish myself with heroic steel!"


scarlet blossom

of the dunes in April's lust

last rose of the heavens


"Crazy! They're uprooting it, now they wipe it so triumphantly on the dirty velvet of a cape. It's horrible to feel life flowing away... Aaaah! Another sword has stabbed me in the back! Sinking in! Aaah!..."


1st terror

2nd terror

To be stitched back together with heroism

BACK TOGETHER

The motionless bull wears a black cross upon his chest, a black sierra.  Out of his slobbering face the badly shaking white tongue hisses
    "With me dies the king of bulls, an antisocial horned machine of exploding savage power!  But before I go, if only my jet of blood could be a fountain...  If it only would double its spurt, I could, yes, uproot this blade and turn it against this damn man with a leap!"


        Andante maestoso



                    redblack

                redblackviolet


    Silence.  Weights and measures of fatality.  To the eyes of an aviator flying 1,000 meters over Barcelona, the bull resembles a mysterious black tear upon a golden dish whose flower-strewn border shimmers in the evening breeze.




        200 kilometers per hour

        7 more risks of rupture

        in the wings' struts

The bull moos,
"Now, now I cannot fix you, smart, repulsive matador
who wouldn't dare fight with me alone.  I dribble all of my
contempt on you, friends to this massacre, and on the idiotic
applause with which you feed your courage.  I see, three
feet away from my right leg, the Enemy of thunderstruck
oak, with a carbon face sculpted by vultures.  I must kill
him!"


(quick crescendo)


Death


While he rattled thus, the bull centered all of his
effort in his sharp horns.  Then, suddenly losing his four
legs as though they had vanished, he fell, a long long
black bomb, against invisible but present Death.
The grinding of entangled horns and bones.  Awful
crumple followed by a pathetic burst from the human
groundwork in the seats of the Arena de toros.


(continuing faster crescendo)


greatgreatviolet

Stillness.  Tortuous anguish.

The sun leaves its orbit and sinks down
the main grandstand steps to get a better
look.   Dazzling staring belly

becomes

the Great Eye

of blackgold

so very slowly

Some music, for God's sake!  A little music, fast!
Out it skips, bursting with trumpets, drums, pipes, like
during all the tranquil festivities of cattle merchants.

1 drum

2 drums and 3 trumpets

11 drums

11 trumpets

11 pipes

1931

## AEROPICTORIAL DINNER IN A COCKPIT

Inside the big cockpit of a great De Bernardi
airship, flying through aeropaintings by the
Futurists Marasco, Tato, Benedetta, Oriani
and Munari, that hang on the peaks and clouds
on the horizon; flying high at one thousand
meters, the passengers free 5 lobsters from
their shells and boil them electrically in
sea water. They stuff them with a batter of
egg-yolks, carrots, thyme, garlic, lemon peel,
lobster eggs, livers and capers. Then they
sprinkle curry powder and put them back inside their shells tinted here and there with
a Mytilene blue.

Then the lobsters are confusedly arranged
upon a great ceramic Tullio d'Albisola mat-
tressed with twenty different salads: these
geometrically set up like checkers.

The dining passengers, seizing ceramic
steeples filled with Barolo wine mixed with
Asti Spumante, eat thus villages factories
and lowlands carried off at great speed.

by Marinetti and Fillia from
                    La cucina futurista, 1932

## SIMULTANEITY OF A NIGHT READY FOR WAR
## AND FACETED WITH EXPLOSIVE PRIDE

If on a hot August night you were to cruise in a
motorboat from Lerici directly to Portovenere the prow
skimming across the motherly curve with its lips the
Milky Way transforms under your young hands in the clear
longing of the ebony basket Gulf whose bottom is filled
with plaited splendors
 Don't watch for the white peep-holes of submarine
parties that fishing boats mimic far away
 Don't watch for the black apparition of a sail
clambering up over your shoulder
 Watch for the searchlight that pierces the zenith
and screams after sweeping the silver sea
 "Thieves thieves full of envy rapacity woe unto him
who denies my triumph in the last full moon of diamond and
mercury when planted upon the gold pilings of my reflections I am proclaimed the most fearful, handsome warship
woe to whomever touches my imperial jewels I'll make them
blow up explode all their ripping white visciousness right
in his face"
 Silent but completely armed with pearl chrome surfaces and vermilion pendants a battle-ship machine-guns
in a continuous rage of magnesium shocking a dark cruiser
into a serious laboratory of scientific lights
 The cruiser doesn't seem to notice too preoccupied with the austere rubies from lighthouses and its
duties to luminous telegraphy
 The magically female, long white hand of another
ship plants her long-nailed ivory fingers into the high
pine grove of Mount Marcello there there yes there and
further in there with the pinching crackle of leaves harps
mandolins awakening some lively sparrows and quintupling
their population yes yes look the sun is rising rising what
the why its no sun maybe the moon or maybe a wild dance
party thrown for fish that escaped the nets and fishing
grounds all floating eels mackerels sardines dentex sea-
perch anchovies mullet millet grain and golden horse dung
from a Sunday street wrong wrong we were dreaming yes let's
go back to sleep yes yes a dream
 Yes
 Patiently regularly from North to South East to West
the searchlights' resplendent compasses resume their measure of distances between the stars and earthly surfaces

depths of images and parabolas of migrant hypotheses
Who can overpower that insurrection of light from
the cruiser that bawls
"Hang me up like the richest chandelier of patriotic
ardor among the presumptuous constellations at the zenith"
The Fleet shines like a trajectory equation beneath
the starlit cupola spinning with a million gunsights
Stars
Heavy truce of the night kneaded together out of
sleep passion envy and provisional death
But the officers and sailors below decks and sleeping have left their fiery hearts on the empty bridge to
keep vigil
And in the center of the flagship a big smoking kitchen of war cooks round tunas and enamoured mouths weeping eyes and fat splendorous torpedoes

from L'Aeropoema del golfo della Spezia, 1935

SIMULTANEITY OF DREAMS AND MORNING ARTILLERY
SHOTS FOR RESHAPING A LANDSCAPE

Cobalt and tactilism of baby chick down

In the fresh soft silky light quilted with little gold
shavings maybe because of this the airplane has such a
soft bra bra bra bra as it dives with open blessing arms
over the pillboxes right and left of the Uarieu strong-
hold

The light makes sculpture more miraculous than the artillery

Thanks to it the soldiers line up to make a black comb
and look like gigantic elongated spectators as three
cannons pour out fluttering cloaks of steel and flames
flapping toom toom toom and the projectiles saaa sraaaa
fraaaa into the silky air and then a very far digested
ploooommmmm

The constantly competitive light polishes Uorcamba to a
double hump of lean observation-posts softening surfaces
and tortuous rocks mixing them with affectionate eternal
concerns picnics on the grass and even the memory of sonorous bells during holidays in the villages

Grrufff  grrufff echoes linger grumbling gruushaaaa
gruushaaaa gruushaaaa  increased gloomy

Cobalt and tactilism of baby chick down

Once the light designs and chisels the blockhouse on
the left the order arrives by telephone
--Cease fire stand ready

A pearly little monkey with an insolent tail settles
upon the heliograph and wants to go on rendering and re-
sculpting the landscape

Suddenly a volley between the conical Coptic church and
spires the airplane wants to focus its fire upon the
slope there are so many Abyssinians in flight

But the flies always insist on readjusting their scorching fire to point-blank

Cobalt and Tactilism of baby chick down


from"Il poema africano della Divisione '28 Ottobre'"
1937

SIMULTANEOUS POETRY OF BUSINESS

AT THE PORT OF GENOA


--Words are enough when the business is conducted
between honest men the Cardiff 20,000 tons a
tannery and two hotels on the coast
--Do you want two deposits of coal
--No my Georgina is six years old beautiful as an
angel but she needs pure air I'm gonna teach her
how to run the hotel closing 2 per cent for you
--You better hurry it up with your insurance if
there are more than thirty broken sacks I don't
know what Liverpool thinks of it but in Genoa we
make no agreements on broken sacks
--Tough business
--Slim business anyhow to show you my benevolence
I'll speak to my friend at the harbormaster's
office
--Or the disaster with the California fruit could
happen again
--That's the way it was after two days of sailing
the Kimura stank like a fish market in the sirocco
--After the Deal we'll talk about the pineapples
my son loads them at Dakar tomorrow they'll sail
along the Balearic coast in a sea of heaven perfumed to please the passengers aboard the Rex
where they'll lick each other's noses like emperors
on those first class decks
--Georgina loves pineapple too at my walled villa
every morning she waits on the terrace before the
windows crammed with fire by the sun
On board my son raises the flag over the bow and
watches Georgina through binoculars as she claps
her hands but I can't lower the price believe me
if this much gives me that much this much will
give him that much leaving only so much for himself and so much lost for that much time
--So much for you Baciccia with all the much that
you make you'll still survive for many years Good
Luck
--The weather is beautiful the ship's purchase is
well bargained sailing like this we're hauling 3
million and not a penny more my second son you know
him even he declares it on paper
--And the tug?
--100,000 lire

--Baciccia only the foam is left for me
--If the foam bothers you we'll go below and have
a drop and finish up


Baciccia's nerves steaming steaming fish scaly
packs of 1,000 lire notes out on a sea all tangled
in bilious unsuccessful deals
Luckily there shines up from the celestial purse
empty till then the first shimmering golden guar-
antee evening star
As sunset continues the Port will throw open its
windows of glossy gold ingots without any risk
He who buys the grieving black velvet of the
nights of love and a good measure of silken furry
speed on his frozen cheeks buys well
Stability in the liquid marketplace of devalued
waves two sailing ships bundled in shadowy
promisorry notes
The farthest under a low cloud cooks the last
sanguine anguish of an irreparable financial day
Hesitation of two other ships with thick tangles
of debts accumulated by the indecisions and
distances under ringing constellations cashed
in by the night
very quickly
The general expenses of the day now forgotten
a shred of tinsel clouds remains
With the tug-boat procured he re-enters the
shining electricity that Genoese wharfs perspire
far onto the horizon thinking that if the sea
were gasoline he could earn in one blow all the
starry well-dressed balances of ambition
consolidated away from charge accounts
--They call me Blackfinger Baciccia here on my
baby finger I have a hardened callus from un-
loading petroleum and fresh chestnuts off the
Langhe it brought me luck when I was in the
Loading Square Bar by the way paid me back well
I slugged the stomachs of five Arabs in their
goat skins from Massaua When I caress Georgina's
cheeks I'd like to burn this thick black callus
off for her not made for coal or a dock-worker
like me she'll stay at the inn in San Remo on
the coast by the pure sea they've poured it off
a hundred times into little silk bags foaming
with luxury everything deluxe even the trees in
the wind always bowing down and historic chamber-

maids who drive dragging a pair of dachshunds fed
on bananas Baciccia's nerves scream entering into
the darkness of the banks with long trains of
bristling and vindictive millions
For hours and hours during the night the Office
pours out into the port all of its lugubrious
circulating greed while the wandering souls of
seated American seances gather like grain in silos.
The promise kept with a word given in a distant
near illusory paid unpayable Leaves only the
commercial Soviet fleet to unload selling off
I will sell them all the spoiled rum from Sotto-
ripa at a high price and to its commissary on
shore I will sell at an outrageous price an auto-
graphed letter from General Cardenas that specifies
to me how to prevent the next three Mexican
revolutions
Baciccia sits in the niche of his balcony window
at San Remo buys and sells over the telephone
twenty smoky oily pieces of the port of Genoa
bubbling in a smoking boiler overcooked while a
slender sun in rose velvet glitters sparkles sets
softly in order to stretch out nearby with the
smoothnesses of mother-of-pearl porcelain green
Africanisms of yellow aloes regimen of date-palm
and the liquid sequins of the exhaling blue sea
Behind him in the immense white bed of her life
Georgina leafs through an atlas sugared with
falling rays
--Hello!  Hello!  coastal station of Genoa Radio
Castellaccio make an offer of 100,000 sacks of
cacao 200,000 sacks of nutmeg 6 cisterns of mineral
oil to the ships Gallipoli Almenara Probitas
Arrange everything I wouldn't take my baby into
the port of Genoa the port is one immense deposit
of dumped tar in fact it's a urinal for trans-
atlantics where one traffics in aromatic shit from
the rest of the world
The port responds with a long low oooo
--Baciccia you're right oooo still higher prices
lowered into the hold and cranes cranes cranes
cranes rotating relaxing on the gluttonous holds
of the night rising out to snowflakes black with
a million icy razors eruptions of seaplanes which
will shortly deal directly with the highest stars
I knooooow it I knooooow it
Over Baciccia's head the warm roses of San Remo
somersault from the balcony terraces drunk on art

and mad with delightfully besieging the palms
embracing them compelling them to dive deeply
into the fluid silver sea that the elastic sun
dazzling kilometric butterfly stretches with
its great gold springs
Millions of carnations explode in their red-hot
greenhouses peppering the air with vermilion
words in support
--What's coal worth what's gasoline worth if
they don't speed up the genius of the earth so
we can pay our bills now Italy exports little
given how every distant land manufactures its
own needs Italy could but prefers to import to
conserve her genius and sentiment therefore we
Italians have an excessive load here that crowds
out-weighs obstructs degrades poisons etcetera
a product declared alive and surely it lives in
its own way unfortunately it trickles ominous
epidemics out of its casings I can recognize
the product by its special smell when it appears
among you baby roses and in the midst of our
fertile population of carnations we fade grow
flabby spite disgust horror rage atrocity
Living yes but an ignoble human product deprived
of eyes a mouth a sense of smell that won't
move nor will it ever be moved by the thoughts-
colors that our perfumes paint upon the air
An opaque product whose temperature remains
fixed while Virgin Poetry melodiously blazes
dances and smiles within a crowd of firesmell
languages
--Baciccia quick sell sell off this product
ship it as soon as it's loaded ship it load it
for exportation in blocks masses mountains
--Close up those crates nail them down and
pack pack them up
--Capacious ships with oceanic holds line your
insides of intelligent mirroring steel and lock
it up above because that wicked stink could
watch out watch out explode
--Run to the plane station and load the seaplanes
too with this vile stuff You will identify it at
customs by these foul words: cretinism pedantry
envy foreignfetishism provincialism passeism
nostalgia already twenty years too old
--Far out at sea seaplanes shit it out and climb
--Oooo Baciccia oooooo Baciccia Bacicciaaa looook
our deal our deal our deal our deeeeal

from Il poema non umano dei tecnicismi, 1940

## SIMULTANEOUS POETRY OF PERNAMBUCO


Delicious voyage from Cairo's crystallized pistachios
camel meat stews upon kitchen spits that I tasted in
Marrakesh to the metal prow of our ship savoring the
sugared rays of the foaming dawn
--Oh delicious sea-sauce gravying our round earthly
fruit  After gazing absent-mindedly at Algerian jetties
and the roads with minarets in turban white and fez red
sunset here is Gibraltar's sumptuous searchlight beam
employed seeking to dazzle ships strongholds darkness
promontories rebels while reports of a diplomat who
escaped Communist bullets in Barcelona and the Fascist
recreation organization who've invited me to speak
about our glorious Africa prepare me to relish like some
thirst-quenching fruit the Brazilian port I am going to
visit
Pernambuco's mechanical and vegetable simultaneity in the
Winter-Summer of August
Our motor-ship Neptune entering slowly as if into an
enemy's bed and the Ocean of finally exhausted yellow
bile compel one hundred metal cranes dressed like giraffes
to hunt and do battle below with the tall feathered tribes
of palms and camerus undressed in the thick fog defeated
sun
Because of the many catarrhs of grating chains and sharp
steam whistles spoiling the cranes' invitations to me
with their hanging mercantile tongues for enjoying the
war between colors and tropical odors
Quickly enjoying a miraculous olfactory landscape
--With my nostrils wide open attentive I can tell the
difference between six grades of the finest tobacco
--That's the smell of toast
--That's coffee
--Cooked sugar
--Ripe bananas
--Jasmine
--Mould
--Puppets' hair in the sun
--Mango
--Ananas
--We call it abacasci a more refreshing Brazilian name
--Meanwhile the rain sputters crackles and washes away
upon the terraces and in the streets where electricity
stretches like swinging coconuts
Negroes all attired with armed innocence and straw hats
of condensed sun wait fearlessly ready at every corner

176

Firing blasting repetitious happiness and thoughtlessness
against the collected dullness of flame smoky clouds
finally set to liquidate the city forever
Fortunately the ritziest autos dripping with beautifully
clear reflections arrive like indispensible reinforce-
ments during war
Perplexity of the battle
Against the bitter flavor horror of the night drenched in
darkness they hurl themselves upon the thick mellifluous
souls of cane sugar troops that besiege the central
districts    A crescendo of tempting sweetness fills the
burnt shops next to one another where they weave together
thirsty velvet watered silk red lamps smoking cigars
jingling glasses filled with lilac and emerald drinks
very carefully negroes with orange silk mantillas upon
their right arms and mulattas whose heads of hair explode
with ribbons and silver combs    Stopping coagulating or
circulating about of small black feet beneath the snowy
bells of linen pantaloons
How I would enjoy shaving my beard like those razor-cut
slices of fruit in an amazing confusion of looking-glasses
and crushing flames
Evidently the three negroes dressed in white before the
shop-window of the largest bar in the city are the command-
ers of the last anti-rainy anti-gray anti-funereal counterattack
Each one in fact is armed with his own smiling ingenious
collar cravat and shirt in the most beautiful gaudy rose
Before I leave I would like to stir up the solitary
breakwater that directly confronts the Ocean and her
flooding sorrows with the luminous and tasty strawberry
sprinkling every five seconds of its portable beacon on
the point overlooking the foamy reefs
While the Neptune starts out from Pernambuco with its
spinning piercing Italian steel far inside the depths
of the immeasurably voluptuous Ocean its long abandon-
ments and thousand thousand thousand rests you denied
Frutta del Conte clearly for him only for his reserved
delight you gracious pinecone continuing to defend with
your silent dark green of wood yet to be profaned by
sunlight unfolded yet between my hands and offered to
me from mouth to mouth your teeth creamy and granulated
with such a sweet white thick sauce of sky and brunette
in love

from Il poema non umano dei technicismi, 1940

## FATHERLY NIGHT

Tepid African night upon a mess-table of
stars in a tent with soup of winds ice and
canned sadnesses

I don't want to play cards or tell little
sidesplitting stories

I need to keep the sentinels awake one
after the other and enjoy again the kisses
of my children in my dream

from Canzoniere futurista
amoroso e guerriero, 1943

## IN A BATHING SUIT

In my bathing suit walking the beach
alongside the sea spindly cool already
far ruddy clouds

talking Fish you shouted to me a good
no of foamy water

Todaytomorrow after a bath of darkness
nightoblivion I'll snatch a gilded yes
of perfume from you on the sly

Daybreak of flesh

Frosty rosetree

Mirthful mine explosion

from Canzoniere futurista
amoroso e guerriero, 1943

DAYBREAK AT TOBRUK

My nightshirt has a spate of little
holes

Fat little holes and sleeves worn out
by amorous rays and aerial bombs

Thus a mother-of-pearl cloud spoke
quietly in rose to the African sun

What a pain if they resume the
fighting tonight

But with his usual cooking the
steaming macho sun cried lover
I'll crush you I'll crush you

And everything lovingly drank up
the cloud radiator blond in the
desert of orange satin

from Canzoniere futurista
amoroso e guerriero, 1943

QUARTER OF AN HOUR OF POETRY
TO THE 10TH E-BOAT SQUADRON
(Music of Feelings)

Climb aboard your trucks aeropoets and be off finally
off to be blessed after so many piercing whistles of
wheels swallows detractors retorts of windy pessimism

Engine breakdown among Italians but you you twenties are
by now the famous resisters from the draft of the Ideal
and I must tell you that often I tried to absolve you
accusing the oppressive pedantry of official paper
bureaucracies restrictions censures formalisms small-
minds and passeism torturers with which they would
bemire the boiling adamantine rhythm of your voluntary
service rising in the middle of the battlefield

I will not cry see you later in Paradise up there where
it will be your turn to obey the purest infinite love
of God while now you rage with the desire of commanding
an army of arguments so move forward trucks

Urbanisms workshops banks and plowed fields you go to
school by these solemn professors of sociology ants
termites bees beavers

World I have nothing to teach you for I am of every
quotidianism and a beacon of an aeropoetry beyond time
space

The cemeteries of great Italians unbutton their small
rural walls in the cowardice of the sirocco and shoot
off sparks crackle with the impatience of powder-
magazines without doubt they will explode they do
explode predatory dead so move on trucks

You pontoonists brakemen of the calculated step you
grave-diggers pig-headed in your effort of burying
Springtimes' enthusiasts of glory tell me you are
satisfied with having been able to plunge straight
to the bottom of your ideological dung-heap the
fragile and delicious Italy wounded undying

Move forward trucks and do not be distracted roll up
your courageous body in shreds which the cruel speed
wishes to send to heaven before its hour

A cemetery of great Italians explodes and cries Stop
stop Italian drivers you'll need explosives and we'll
give them to you we'll give them us us the best explosives extracted from the marrow of our skeletons

And it may be the word bones rhymes with the word power
in ancient verse fragments nostrils of the Future
excited by the ripening hay-smell of supremacy

Here we are finally descending to almost holy ground

Rugged beatitude of hills made fierce they rip open

The voluptuous first line of combat vibrates like long
stretched strings that the projectiles strum a thundering cathedral lying down to implore Jesus with pangs
of lacerated breasts

We will be we are the kneeling machine-guns with barrels
trembling in prayer

I kiss and kiss again the spiked weapons with a thousand
thousand thousand hearts all pierced by the vehement
eternal oblivion

1944

O Beny
blessed water!
Dear hawthorn
with the red eyelet
(blood of bilge
and of flesh in war!)
that I am

O Beny
Blessed water
fallen from the moon
this soft holy water stoup
of Christian nights!

Legend?  History?  Who knows?
Once on the banks of an emerald river
some converted natives
(crazy with music)
constructed
a church
out of bamboo
mystical and warm
exquisite twilight
where sinks
the brutal caress of the Sun

The missionary with rosy cheeks
in his old greenish robes
says the Mass sweats and sighs
drinking a cool wine
out of a tender piece of sugar-cane
Wine of the good Lord,
its coolness
in the throats of the damned
worth dying for!

But a holy water stoup is needed
for all the natives in the land!
A gigantic coconut is needed
And there they are climbing up
over the highest palms
The largest nut
so the legend says
was alas too small!
for their propagandistic desire

A native let
these words
fall from above:
--As for me I only sculpt
the infinite fruits of Paradise!
The palm with its native on top
bends down to the ground like a catapult
The surroundings are deforested
Suddenly straightening up
the tree hurls the native artist away
like a heavy black speck
into the lovely serene night
And the native reached
his distant
coconut
from the forest in Paradise
with which to make his stoup!

Beny blessed water
who overflows
from the nocturnal stoup
moon or coconut
fruit of Paradise!
Beny clear light
quenching
Beny crib of my heart-Jesus
cool
breach
in my millenarian shadows
Divine milk
from my rough half-shell
my
nut
of your coco

from Poesie a Beny, 1971

# SELECTED BIBLIOGRAPHY

Works by F. T. Marinetti:

La conquête des étoiles, poeme epique. Paris, 1902.

Enquête internationale sur le Vers Libre et manifeste du futurisme. Milan, 1901.

Destruction, poèmes lyriques. Paris, 1904.

La ville charnelle. Paris, 1908.

Le Futurisme. Theories et mouvement. Paris, 1911.

Le monoplan du pape, roman politique en vers libre. Paris, 1912.

La bataille de Tripoli (26 Octobre 1911) vecue et chantee par F. T. Marinetti. Milan, 1912.

I poeti futuristi con una proclama di F. T. Marinetti e uno studio sul verso libero di Paolo Buzzi. Milan, 1912.

Versi e prose di S. Mallarmé, trans. F. T. Marinetti. Milan, 1916.

Zang tumb tumb, Adrianopoli Ottobre 1912, parole in liberta. Milan, 1914.

Scelta di poesia e parole in libertà. Milan, 1918.

8 anime in una bomba, romanzo esplosivo. Milan, 1919.

Les mots en liberté futuristes. Milan, 1919.

Gli indomabili. Milan, 1922.

I nuovi poeti futuristi. Milan, 1925.

Primo dizionario aereo. Milan, 1929.

Spagna veloce e toro futurista, poema parolibero. Milan, 1931.

Il fascino dell'Egitto. Milan: Mondadori, 1933.

L'aeropoema del golfo della Spezia. Milan: Mondadori, 1935.

Il poema Africano della divisione "28 Ottobre." Milan: Mondadori, 1937.

Il poema non umano dei tecnicismi. Milan: Mondadori, 1940.

Canzoniere futurista amoroso e guerriero, versi e musiche. Savona: Istituto Grafico Brizio, 1943.

Quarto d'ora di poesia della X Mas (musica di sentimenti). ed. Benedetta Marinetti. Milan: Mondadori, 1945.

186

_Teoria e invenzione futurista_. ed. Luciano De Maria, Milan: Mondadori, 1968.

_La grande Milano tradizionale e futurista. Una sensibilita Italiana nata in Egitto_. ed. Luciano De Maria, Milan: Mondadori, 1969.

_Poesie a Beny_. Turin: Einaudi, 1971.

_Selected Writings_. ed. R.W. Flint, trans. R.W. Flint and Arthur A. Coppotelli. New York: Farrar, Straus and Giroux, 1972.

_Scritti francesi_. ed. Pasquale A Jannini. Milan: Mondadori, 1983.

_Autoportrait et les amours futuristes par F. T. Marinetti_. ed. Gérard-Georges Lemaire. Paris: Centre Georges Pompidou, 1984.


Selected Studies:

Apollonio, Umbro, ed. _Futurist Manifestos (Documents of 20th Century Art)_. New York: Viking, 1973.

Bartolucci, Giuseppe. _Il gesto futurista_. Rome: Bulzoni, 1969.

Benedetto, Enzo, ed. _Marinetti domani: convegno di studi nel primo centenario della nascita di F. T. Marinetti_. Rome: Arte Viva, 1977.

Bergman, Par. _"Modernalatria" et "Simultaneita"_. Stockholm: Bonnier, 1962.

Crispolti, Enrico. _Il secondo futurismo_. Turin: Pozzo, 1961.

----------. _Il mito della macchina e altri temi del futurismo_. Trapani: Celebes, 1969.

De Maria, Luciano. _Per conoscere Marinetti e il futurismo_. Milan: Mondadori, 1973.

De Micheli, Mario. _La matrice ideologico-letteraria dell' eversione fascista_. Milan: Feltrinelli, 1976.

Drudi Gambillo, M. and T. Fiori. _Achivi del futurismo_. Rome: De Luca. vol.1, 1958; vol. 2, 1962.

Eruli, Brunella. "Bibliografia delle opere di F. T. Marinetti (1898-1909)," _La Rassegna della letteratura italiana_, no. 2-3 (March-December 1968) pp. 368-388.

----------. "Preistoria Francese del futurismo," _Rivista di letterature moderne e comparate_, no. 23 (1970), pp. 245-290.

Gherarducci, Isabella, ed. Il futurismo italiano. Rome: Riuniti, 1976.

Jacobbi, Ruggero. "Per una rilettura della poesia futurista e nota sulla narrativa futurista," Poesia e critica, no. 8-9 (May 1966).

--------. Poesia futurista italiana. Parma: Guanda, 1968.

Joll, James. "F. T. Marinetti--Futurism and Fascism," Three Intellectuals in Politics. New York: Pantheon, 1960.

Kirby, Michael. Futurist Performance, with Manifestos and Playscripts translated from the Italian by Victoria Nes Kirby. New York: Dutton, 1971.

Lambiase, Sergio and G. Battista Nazzaro. Marinetti e i futuristi: Marinetti nei colloqui e nei ricordi dei futuristi italiani. Milan: Garzanti, 1978.

Lista, Giovanni. Marinetti. Paris: Seghers, 1976.

Mariani, Gaetano. Il primo Marinetti. Florence: Le Monnier, 1970.

Martin, Marianne W. Futurist Art and Theory. Oxford: Clarendon Press, 1968.

Nazzaro, Gian Battista. Introduzione al futurismo. Naples: Guida, 1973.

Paglia, Luigi. Invito alla lettura di Filippo Tommaso Marinetti. Milan: Mursia, 1977.

Peirone, Luigi. Lo strumento espressivo di Marinetti. Genoa: Tilgher, 1976.

Romani, Bruno. Dal simbolismo al futurismo. Florence: Sandron, 1969.

Rye, Jane. Futurism. London: Dutton, 1972.

Sanzin, Bruno G. "Omaggio a Benedetta Marinetti," Il ragguaglio librario. 44 (1977), pp. 371-74.

Scrivo, Luigi. Sintesi del futurismo (storia e documenti). Rome: Bulzoni, 1968.

Silingardi, Germana. "Alcuni modi della metafora marinettiana in Zang tumb tumb." Verri 13-16 (1979) pp. 224-54.

Silva, Umberto. Ideologia e arte del fascismo. Milan: Mazzotta, 1973.

Verdone, Mario. Cinema e letteratura del futurismo. Rome: Bianco e nero, 1968.

--------. Prosa e critica futurista. Milan: Feltrinelli, 1973.

Peter N. Pedroni

# Existence as Theme in Carlo Cassola's Fiction

American University Studies: Series II (Romance Languages and Literature), Vol. 31
ISBN 0-8204-0236-2          191 pp.          hardback          US $ 26.65*

*Recommended price - alterations reserved

Despite his early reputation as a neorealist, Cassola's themes were existential and his purpose was always to express existential emotions – the feeling of awe in the contemplation of the importance of the opposite sex as a catalyst to active participation in life, the mysterious ways in which a life's destiny is determined, the irrevocable passing of time with its inherent sense of loss, the fundamental sadness caused by the necessity of death, and joy in the acceptance of existence as an absolute value in itself. The material that he used to express these emotions ranges from everyday life in small town Italy to action-filled combat scenes based on his own experiences as a partisan fighter during World War II.

Cassola's fiction offers the reader an unusually clear perspective of the complexities of contemporary Italian society and of the relationship of the individual to that society.

Contents: The Early Fiction – The Post-War Period – The So-called Neorealist Phase – The Return to the Youthful Poetics – The Early 1970s.

PETER LANG PUBLISHING, INC.
62 West 45th Street
USA – New York, NY 10036

Zeitfracht Medien GmbH
Ferdinand-Jühlke-Straße 7
99095 Erfurt, Deutschland
produktsicherheit@kolibri360.de

Druck:
CPI Druckdienstleistungen GmbH
im Auftrag der
Zeitfracht Medien GmbH
Ein Unternehmen der Zeitfracht - Gruppe
Ferdinand-Jühlke-Str. 7
99095 Erfurt